Dear Papa

By Sam Wilson, courtesy of Flying Spur Press

Dear Papa

Letters Between John Muir
And His Daughter Wanda

Edited and Documented
by
Jean Hanna Clark
and
Shirley Sargent

Panorama West Books
Fresno, California
in cooperation with
Flying Spur Press
Yosemite, California

Library of Congress Card Catalog Number 85-060103
International Standard Book Number 0-914330-76-4

Manufactured in the United States of America

Contents

Foreword

Among nature-lovers and conservationists, the name John Muir is a household word. Today his admirers visit Muir Woods and the John Muir National Historic Site in northern California, wander through the Muir Grove and the Muir Wilderness Area in Sequoia National Park, hike through the Muir Gorge in Yosemite National Park, or tramp the John Muir Trail on the backbone of the Sierra Nevada. On it is the nearly 12,000-foot Muir Pass and a conical rock shelter called the Muir Hut. Hardy backpackers ascend 14,000-foot Mount Muir from which they can see Muir Lake. There is a Muir Crest, a Muir Beach, and in southern California, a Muir Peak.

California, Muir's home from 1868 until his death in 1914, has more sites commemorating him than any other person. In and near his hometown of Martinez are the John Muir National Historic Site, a John Muir Wilderness area, a parkway, a hospital, and numerous commercial establishments bearing his name. Throughout the United States there are many "John Muir" schools, and Wisconsin has a 160-acre John Muir County Park surrounding his leafy boyhood haunts. His Scottish birthplace boasts a John Muir Country Park. Another mighty scenic memorial is the Muir Glacier in Alaska.

Because of these sites and the many books by and about him, millions of people, not only in America but throughout the world, are aware of Muir's achievements and importance as a pioneer conservationist and champion of the wilds. Thousands know his still-influential ringing, singing words. Hundreds collect his books, quote passages, and follow his advice to "get them [the mountains] into your hearts so at length their preservation and right use might be made sure." Only a scattering of devotees, however, know of Muir's private life and his role as a devoted though unconventional family man.

In this book, through a documented compilation of letters between him and his elder daughter Wanda, Muir emerges as humorous, instructive, infinitely tender, and sometimes chauvinistic. He spent more than half his life as a bachelor, but his commitment to marriage, at the age of 42, was as whole-hearted as his earlier commitment to "show forth the beauty, grandeur and all-embracing usefulness" of nature.

Even in his most footloose years as a self-styled tramp, he labored in fields, farms, and a factory to support himself, as well as help his seven sisters and brothers with their education. He was ever loyal and generous to his family, including his fanatically religious father. Muir's bachelorhood may well have been prolonged because of his keen memories of Daniel Muir as an oppressive, tyrannical father. Unlike Daniel, John himself became a loving husband and adoring father.

Friends and family were delighted when John came down from the mountains, literally and figuratively, on April 14, 1880, to be married. His wife, Louie Wanda, was the only child of Louisiana and John Strentzel. He was a Polish exile and a physician, well-known for his success in horticulture. Louie was no dewy-eyed maid, but a mature and competent woman of 33, who helped her aging father supervise, and keep the books for, his 2,665-acre ranch. While attending a private high school in Benicia, she had become a skilled pianist and following graduation was asked to give concerts. She spurned them as she did marriage proposals, preferring to stay at home with her parents.

The Strentzel home was a two-story Dutch Colonial house surrounded by hills, orchards, and vineyards in the Alhambra Valley south of Martinez. As a wedding gift, the Strentzels turned the house and twenty acres over to the newlyweds. The older couple shared it for two years while their seventeen-room Victorian "mansion" was being built a mile north. John Muir labored in the fields, learning all aspects of raising grapes and fruit trees. He was hard-working, thrifty, and creative, which impressed the Strentzels. However, Muir took off for Alaska while the grapes ripened in late summer. This shocked neighbors and friends, but it was a pre-nuptial agreement worked out between the Muirs. Louie knew that mountains were essential to his physical and emotional well-being. Each immersion in them led to renewed productivity that could benefit mountains and mankind. She must have been aware of people's critical talk regarding Muir's periodic desertions, but because she understood his needs so well, she never held him back. Only once, early in their marriage when he was in Alaska, did she betray her needs in forlorn letters. Otherwise their personal correspondence is a testimony to her understanding and to their love, which was strong and abiding.

Only once did Louie accompany him, and that was on an 1884 trip to Yosemite Valley. After that she remained at home by choice, helping her parents, taking care of the accounts, and exchanging frequent letters with her husband. Her health was never robust, a fact that he fretted about in his letters, which she treasured. Her frailness, probably a chronic problem, might have kept her from joining him, but she was not an invalid or a complainer. Louie was ever the mainstay of the Muir family, a contented homebody.

On March 25, 1881, Muir wrote a friend, "I am now the happiest man in the world." His letter went on to announce the birth of his firstborn, Annie Wanda Muir: "We are five now—four steadfast old lovers around one little love."

The arrival of a second daughter, Helen, on January 23, 1886, was equally joyful, but her hold on life seemed so tenuous there was more anxiety than ecstasy. Muir was so concerned for her that he made no long trips until she was walking and talking. No matter where he went or how difficult it was to write, whether on mountain peaks or during blizzards, Muir penned letter after letter to his beloved wife and "bairns."

Not only did his body and spirit require weeks and months exploring mountains and glaciers, but his career as a writer and leader in the emerging conservationist movement demanded such absences from home. "Oh Papa, when are you coming home?," the reiterated plaint in Wanda's letters, could have been a title for this book. His many letters to the girls and, more so, to his wife, expressed a constant concern for their welfare. Be careful of fire, take particular care with candles, cover yourselves with mosquito netting . . . were some of his admonitions. His longing for them was equally expressed.

What good times ensued when he was home! "Father [was] the biggest, jolliest child of us all," Wanda said. What stories he told. The girls heard about Stickeen long before that brave little dog became the hero of one of Muir's most popular books. And what a natural and enthusiastic teacher he was. Inevitably his main subject was nature, "taught" in walks, in comments, even in letters. Soon his receptive daughters shared his affection and appreciation for outdoor marvels. By example and remark, he instructed them to observe, think, and study. They learned verses of his beloved Bobby Burns, for Muir often quoted him in his broadest Scots. Laughter and love were integral to their daily lives.

Wanda and Helen prized their times with Papa, their walks and romps and, when he was away, his letters. They, their mother, and succeeding Muirs preserved most of them, which are now safeguarded by the Holt-Atherton Pacific Center for Western Studies at the University of the Pacific in Stockton, California. Before the bequest, Wanda's daughter, Jean Hanna Clark, the only girl among Muir's ten grandchildren, sifted, sorted, and began to edit the correspondence contained in *Dear Papa*. Only a handful of family letters had been published earlier by William Frederic Badé and Linnie Marsh Wolfe.

Jean was born after her grandfather's death, but grew up in the house that had been his home for the first decade of his marriage. Her older brothers and her parents often talked about Grampa, and the home was so replete with his pictures, books and memorabilia that she felt as if she had known him. Jean had the imagination and ability to begin to collect and edit the correspondence between her mother and grandfather. She believed this enterprise would serve as an unforgettable and enduring portrait of an engaging daughter, and of a man whose greatness as a public servant is well-known, but whose role as a family man had never been revealed.

Jean's career as confidential secretary to the governor of Nevada was so demanding and time-consuming that she asked me to be the editor. Unfortunately, the book was not completed before her death of cancer in January, 1976, and, dismayingly, a number of the original letters used in this book were lost thereafter and so the copies which she made are unique to this publication.

Muir's letters to Helen are equally numerous, and document a strong father-daughter relationship, which, to this editor, shows a partiality to Helen. Once the girls were teenagers, when Wanda showed the independent spirit that made her, Muir said, "unstoppable as an avalanche," his preference for the often sickly, more docile Helen seems unmistakable. My opinions were derived from my study of scores of letters in the Muir Papers at the University of the Pacific. Jean Clark had reached the same conclusion after research and talks with her mother.

Helen needed extra attention, and Wanda was expected to help supply it. She did so lovingly and uncomplainingly even at the sacrifice of graduation from college.

This book unfortunately does not contain all the letters Muir wrote to his daughters over the years. Some have undoubtedly been lost, others—particularly those to Helen—are unavailable for publication. Despite the lack of a complete father-daughters documentation, the following Wanda-Muir exchanges possess an entity, spontaneity, and freshness of their own. The imbalance of chapter lengths was caused by the varying number of letters fitting my time sequence of Wanda's development until her marriage.

John Muir consistently abbreviated the word "and" and often misspelled "Mamma." His punctuation and paragraphing were a bit haphazard, too. No wonder. These were personal letters written without a thought of readers outside his family. Occasionally Wanda's spelling ("Bamph" for Banff) reveals her youth.

It is with pleasure and pride that I edited, and now dedicate, *Dear Papa*, as a memorial to Jean Hanna Clark, a lady of whom her grandfather would have been proud, and one whom I cherished.

Shirley Sargent
Flying Spur, January 1985

Acknowledgements

As already acknowledged, I had every kind of aid and support from Jean Clark. Her brother Dick Hanna, son Ross deLipkau, daughter Isabel Gaines, and sister-in-law Sherry Hanna have also been supportive. Margaret Swett Plummer, granddaughter of Muir's friend John Swett, has been a tower of strength. Her family background and her current work, at a zestful 83, as a ranger-interpreter at the John Muir National Historic Site in Martinez make her an invaluable advisor.

The Muir-Hanna family chose the Holt-Atherton Pacific Center for Western Studies as depository for the Muir papers. Its director, Dr. Ronald Limbaugh, has been a friendly and excellent critic. His assistant, Kirsten Lewis, has helped me in finding letters and photographs. Virginia Reid, of the San Joaquin Valley Information Service in Fresno, assisted with documentation as did Mary Vocelka of the Yosemite Research Library. Noted Muir scholars Maymie and Bill Kimes shared dates and data with me. Barbara W. Billeter was another helpful critic, as were Ann Matteson and Hank Johnson, my sharp-eyed partner in Flying Spur Press. Additional appreciation goes to my patient, nimble-fingered typists, Karen Wood and Raye Santos, to Anne Otto and Connie Holland, who read and reread proofs, and to my enthusiastic publisher Steve Emanuels and his highly capable assistant Doris Hall. Any omissions, errors, or maverick commas are mine, not theirs!

Shirley Sargent
Flying Spur

Holt-Atherton Pacific Center for Western Studies

Muir's sole granddaughter, Jean Hanna Clark (1919-1976), pictured with his famed "study desk" which the family gave to his alma mater, the University of Wisconsin. This book was her inspiration, and is dedicated in memory of her.

Introduction

By Jean Hanna Clark[1]

I grew up knowing that my grandfather Muir was an extraordinary man. My childhood home in Martinez was the very house in which he had married my grandmother and lived for ten years. Naturalist, geologist, conservationist, botanist, explorer, author, and inventor, he was the person whose ideas influenced much of the world's conservation philosophy. He was born on April 21, 1838, in Dunbar, Scotland. His mother, Anne Gilrye, was a descendant of the old Scotch family of Gilderoy. His father, Daniel Muir, was a grain-merchant, a store-keeper, and a religious zealot. John was the third child in the family of three boys and five girls: Margaret, Sarah, John, David, Daniel, Jr., Mary and Annie who were twins, and Joanna. Even as a child, John, though a notable tease, was a protective, loving brother.

In 1849, Daniel Muir sailed for America with three of his oldest children, David, Sarah, and John. They settled in the northern Wisconsin wilderness near Fountain Lake, a few miles from Portage. A man of the time, Father Muir thought all the wild land had to be tamed, and used his children to fell trees, blast stumps, haul rocks, dig a well, plow and plant while he erected a log hut. After his wife and the other children arrived, a two-story hilltop home was built.

Father Muir did more directing than sharing the toil. His obsession was preparing and giving lengthy, dour sermons. Scarcely a moment was spared for the children's schooling from their exhausting, dawn-to-dark farm labor. Somehow, John read every book he

1. Mrs. Clark wrote this introduction in 1972. Since then, minor changes have been made by the editor.

could borrow from neighbors, and so became acquainted with the works of Milton, Shakespeare, Burns, Plutarch's Lives, and Sir Walter Scott. Only in the cold, pre-dawn hours did his father allow him "free" time for study, in the frigid cellar. While the family slept, John studied, worked with tools, and at the same time developed a lifelong hardihood toward cold and discomfort.

As he grew older his mechanical brilliance was demonstrated by ingenious inventions of labor-saving farming devices, including millwheels, barometers, thermometers, and a sawmill. He devised mechanisms that would light a lamp, kindle a fire, and tip him out of bed! His high, three-legged desk whisked books into position for study at pre-programmed times. Intrigued neighbors were so impressed by the talent of this self-taught country boy they persuaded him to enter his inventions at the State Fair in Madison, Wisconsin. After viewing the unique exhibits, a professor encouraged Muir to enroll at the University of Wisconsin. As a special student, he was gloriously happy studying literature, botany, chemistry, and geology. He made influential friends, particularly Professor Ezra Carr and his wife Jeanne, who greatly influenced his life.

He left college to earn money to finance further studies in medical school, but an accident in a factory negated that goal. A steel particle pierced his right eye, and he spent weeks in a darkened room threatened with blindness. Upon recovery, he determined to be true to himself by storing his mind "with the Lord's beauty," and set out on his famous one-thousand mile walk to the Gulf of Mexico. After a long bout with malaria, and a brief sojourn in Cuba, he took steerage passage for California, landing in San Francisco on March 28, 1868. His sole purpose was to visit the already famous Yosemite Valley about which he had heard.

On foot he headed straight for the Sierra Nevada which became his passion and home. For nearly ten years he made Yosemite Valley his headquarters, earning his way as a sheepherder, a sawmill tender, a carpenter, a turkey feeder, and a tourist guide. A generous portion of his pay was sent home to help educate his sisters and brothers. No job was too menial if he could live in the "sanctum sanctorum of the Sierra" where he could observe and absorb nature even while working. He discovered living glaciers, and was the first to recognize and describe glacial forces as being largely responsible for the valley's formation.

As he tramped through the mountains he was dismayed by the

ever-increasing devastation of public lands caused by sheep and cattlemen, lumbermen, and miners. Ancient Sequoias were felled to make lumber. The face of the Sierra was being mutilated through greed and ignorance, and there was no one to protest. John Muir wrote articles urging strong government control of forests and warning that their destruction meant droughts, floods, soil erosion, and agricultural ruin.

Thus, Yosemite, which had given him beauty as well as bread, gave him purpose and lifework as well. He was, he said, hopelessly and forever a mountaineer.

In 1874 Jeanne Carr introduced John Muir to a charming and talented young woman, Louie Wanda Strentzel. He was 36, and she 27. Mrs. Carr had written to Louie earlier stating, "I want you to know my John Muir—and I wish I could give him to some young noble woman 'for keeps,' and so take him out of the wilderness into the society of his peers." Louie was the Texas-born daughter of Louisiana Erwin and John Theophile Strentzel, he a Polish exile, a physician and pioneer horticulturist in Alhambra Valley, just south of Martinez, California. Muir's periodic visits to the hospitable ranch home of the Strentzels culminated in his engagement to Louie Wanda. Mrs. Strentzel documented the occasion in her diary entry of June 17, 1879:

> Yesterday evening Louie and Mr. Muir became engaged for life. Papa and I had retired, when about 1 o'clock Louie came to me, overcome with emotion, threw her arms around me and said, O, Mother, all is well, all is well. She then went away, and I awakened Papa and told him all . . . This morning we all arose with thankful hearts. I wondered if there ever were four happier people than we . . . Mr. Muir is the only man that the Dr. and I have ever felt we could take into our family as one of us and he is the only one that Louie has ever loved, altho she has had many offers of marriage . . .

On April 14, 1880, John and Louie were married in the Strentzel home. Dr. Strentzel's wedding gift to the couple was the house and a portion of the Alhambra Valley ranch which he had planted in vineyards and orchards. Purposefully, John settled down to domestic life and ranching, buying and renting additional land, plunging into the business of scientific horticulture with his native ingenuity and energy.

Within a few months he wrote drolly to a sister, "We expect a long visit from a relative of the family that will no doubt claim a good deal of my time . . . " That exacting relative arrived on March 25, 1881. "Our dear little baby . . . " transformed John o' the Mountains into a proud and ecstatic father at 43, an age when many men were already grandfathers. His delight was obvious in a letter of announcement to his mother, the first of the personal and meaningful letters that comprise this book.

Jean Hanna Clark
Carson City, Nevada, 1972

I

"Our darling firstborn . . ."

Martinez, California,
March 27, 1881

Dear Mother,

Our dear little baby has come to us. She was born just two days ago, March 25 at 2 o'clock in the afternoon, eleven months & eleven days after our marriage, and we are all very happy, father, mother, grandfather, & grandmother [Strentzel], & I am sure that you [Grandmother Muir] will join in our joy.

Our darling firstborn[1] is a tiny, healthy happy daintily featured lassie not at all dull and lumpish like most of the baby garblings that I have seen. She looks about her with her bright blue eyes as steadily as if she were a year old instead of only two days. And her cheeks & brow & mouth & nose & dimpled chin are as finely modelled & composed as if she were in her ripe teens. Heaven bless her & make all her life as happy & loveful as the promise in every quarter is now.

The weather is warm & tranquil & the sun is beaming lovingly on the green hills & blossoming orchards about our home, & the larks & linnets are singing in full springtime chorus. How beautiful the world is, & how beautiful is the time of the coming of our little love. You remember that it was bloomtime of the year when we were married, & our little bloombud baby has arrived in the midst of the

---

1. "Our darling firstborn" was named Annie Wanda for Grandmother Muir, and her mother, Louie Wanda.

richest bloom of the orchards. The cherry trees in particular are one mass of white petals looking as if laden with fleecy snow, while the purple & rose flowers of the quince & peach & apple trees, & the white of the plum is hardly less showy & lavishly abundant.

A happier pair of grandparents than the two Strentzels never was since the beginning of the baby begetting period on earth. How glad we would be to have her Muir grandmother & father here also all four in a ring—a love-ring of steadfast old lovers around this one little love. I want to carry her to you at once, but though that may not be I feel sure that you will see her before long. In the meantime dear Mother send her your love & blessing & forward this letter to father so that our little darling may have his blessing also.[1]

Louie bravely endured her sore mother pains, twelve hours of them, without scarce an audible groan, and has already forgotten them all in her joy.

Ever lovingly your son,

John Muir

•

Despite his euphoria, Alaska called and, before Wanda was two months old, Muir was aboard a ship on an important voyage of exploration. At first he had been reluctant to leave, which pleased the Strentzels, but Louie had argued in private that he needed the trip for the sake of his health and work. Soon his health and zest were abundant as were his letters to his wife which exhibited love and loneliness. "Oh, if I could touch my baby and thee!" "A thousand kisses . . . " "Ah, you little know the long icy days, strangely nightless, that I have longed and longed for one word from you." That was the time when Louie's needs were the greatest. What letters Muir did receive were full of her longing for him.

After that journey, and the resultant writing, Muir again tackled the job of fruit-raising which involved clearing, planting, grafting, pruning, supervising a labor force of thirty or more, harvesting and selling the produce. In all these tasks and others the versatile, hard-working, canny Scot was successful, proving himself to be a fine horticulturist, and also amassing considerable savings. His Bartlett pears and Tokay grapes commanded the best prices. That did not endear him to area ranchers who were also quick to criticize his

1. Daniel Muir's religious fanaticism had led him to Canada where he was happy preaching in the streets and visiting hospital patients. (*Son of the Wilderness*, Linnie March Wolfe, p. 167.)

Louie Strentzel before her marriage.

absences from home. Neither profit nor prophet gained honor in Martinez.

The fact that he went off without his wife garnered more censure, some of which lingers in Martinez today. As noted earlier, Louie Muir did not share her husband's enthusiasm and enjoyment of travel. She was content at home, and needed its comforts and conveniences. Nevertheless, in 1884, when Muir needed a vacation, but refused to leave the ranch, Louie talked him into taking her to Yosemite Valley. Three-year-old Wanda was left with the Strentzels in their new home, and yet her devoted parents spent much of their brief absence fretting about her. It was from Yosemite that John Muir wrote the first of scores of letters to his daughter.

•

Yosemite Valley,
July 10th, 1884.

My dear little Wanda,

Mamma & Papa got the two nice letters that you wrote & Mamma & Papa are very glad because the letters said that you were all right & not crying at all & waiting like a good girl & a sweet baby for Mamma and Papa to come home. & we are coming home soon to our own sweet baby. Mamma and Papa got on the cars & the poogh poogh pulled us to Stockton & there are many mosquitoes in Stockton & they stung Mamma & wouldn't let her sleep. & then we got on to the cars again & another poogh poogh pulled us to Milton and Milton is a very hot place & we were all wet with sweat.[1] & then we came out of the cars & got into a big buggy and six brown horses with long tails trotted fast & galloped some of the time & pulled us to Copperopolis and then the horses were tired & the man that was driving them put them in the stables & gave them a drink of water & some hay to eat & some barley & got some more horses to pull the buggy to a funny looking little town & its name is Chinese Camp.[2] & then the horses got tired again & they were all dusty & wet with sweat & so the man put them in the stable and gave them some water & hay & barley & then the poor things were all right. & just

1. Milton, in Calaveras County, was the terminus of the Stockton and Copperopolis Railroad from 1871 until 1940. For many years it was the staging start for the Calaveras Grove of Big Trees and Yosemite Valley.

2. Copperopolis, Chinese Camp, Big Oak Flat and Crocker's Station were the other main stops on the Big Oak Flat stage road. Although Muir didn't specify overnight stops, they probably spent one night at Chinese Camp and the next at Crocker's.

now a man came to Papa when he was writing this letter & said, "Is this Mr. Muir," and Papa said, "yes." & then the man gave Papa a little letter from Grandpa & the letter said "All well, do not hurry down." & then more horses pulled the buggy up & down many big hills through many bushes with pretty flowers on them & big trees with beautiful cones hanging on the branches & we saw many squirrels with long tails & the squirrels were afraid of the horses & so they ran fast up the trees & began to bark like Bruno, & shake their long tails, but they did not bark so loud as Bruno, & some of the squirrels were gray & some of them had yellow stomachs & they all had whiskers & bright shining eyes, & we couldn't catch them & sometimes we jumped out of the buggy to gather pretty flowers that were growing under the big trees & here is one of the trees, & here is one of the flowers,

& here is one of the squirrels.

Muir Papers, Holt-Atherton Pacific Center for Western Studies

And then we came to Yosemite Valley, & the horses stopped & Mamma and Papa jumped out of the buggy & went into a big house to live til we got home but the people in the big house did not give us anything good to eat, & the bread was sour & the butter too old to eat & the meat was tough & the tea & coffee very bad & so we came away to another big house & we get many good things to eat now & we wish baby could come too & see the pretty flowers & the big trees & the white water falling far down out of the sky.[1] But baby will come with Mamma & Papa some other time when she is a little bigger. This morning the man that keeps the big house that we are living in brought about 20 little fishes all covered with pretty red & yellow spots for Mamma to look at & Mamma said to the man that had the fishes, "Are these catfish" and the man said "no these are trout" & that made Papa laugh for catfish have beards & whiskers and trout have no whiskers but Mamma did not know that. Then the man fried the trout & brought them to us to eat for our breakfast, & he brought some ice-cream too for our breakfast & Papa said to Mamma, "What a funny breakfast this is ice-cream & catfish instead of mush & milk but we had mush & milk too & venison & mutton & ham & eggs & bread. But the funniest things were the little spotted fishes & the ice-cream. An Indian man with long black hair, who never washed his face caught the fishes in a big creek that people call the Merced River. A little boy that lives here has a funny little tiny donkey that has long ears & big sleepy eyes & the boy climbs up on the donkeys back & whips him & makes him trot trot trot up & down the valley & the boy never falls off & everybody looks at the donkey because it looks so little & funny. There are many mules here too & horses & cows & some queer little dogs, & quails & robins & owls. & they make a loud noise some times neighing & lowing & braying & barking & singing & piping but the falling water coming down . . . sings the loveliest song of all . . .

Yosemite Valley
July 16th 1884.

My dear Wanda:

Papa & Mamma are coming home to baby tomorrow & Mamma & Papa have been glad all the time when Grandpa wrote a letter &

1. Since Muir's culinary taste was indifferent, the dinner at Barnard's Hotel, formerly Hutchings House, must have been wretched. The Muirs moved the next day into Leidig's Hotel where Isabella Leidig was well known for providing excellent meals. Muir's friendship with her and her husband, Fred, dated back to the early 1870's when they had all been living in the Yosemite Valley.

baby wrote a letter that said "baby is well & good & does not cry at all" After Papa wrote the other letter to baby Mamma & Papa climbed up a high mountain & Mamma got tired & so Papa walked behind & pushed Mamma with a long stick this way & the stick soon began to hurt Mamma's back & then Mamma was too warm & so she took off some of her clothes & Papa tied a skirt on the end of the stick & then it did not hurt any more.

And when we were about half way up the mountain a man came up behind us with a horse and he said How do you do Mr. Muir and I said "pretty well, this lady is Mrs. Muir, Mr. McCauley" & then he jumped down off his horse & said to Mamma "Please get on my horse Mrs. Muir" & there was a big mans saddle on the horse & some big bags that are called saddle bags & some meat & things in the bags but Mamma got on the top of it all & she looked very funny when she rode away up the mountain with the man behind with a stick whipping the horse to make him go fast.[1]

And when we went to the top of the mountain we were hungry & the man gave us a good dinner & we looked off the top of the mountain & saw many beautiful waterfalls & trees & snow & rocks, & then we climbed up the side of another mountain & when we were climbing up Papa saw the marks of a bears foot & then Mamma was afraid but Papa said the bear is only looking for berries & will not bite. &

1. James McCauley had built the Four-Mile-Trail to Glacier Point in 1871-1872, which the Muirs climbed. McCauley ran the Mountain House on Glacier Point from about 1875 to 1897.

then we told the man about the bear & the man said that an Indian saw the bear about half an hour before. & Mamma was afraid when she was picking flowers for the baby, & Papa has many stories to tell baby. & he & Mamma are coming home tomorrow.

•

Since Muir's formal schooling had been scant and discipline harsh, he evolved new ideas for Wanda's education. "More wide knowledge, less arithmetic and grammar, keeps the heart alive, nourishes youth's enthusiasms . . . " he felt. One of tiny Wanda's first lessons in "nature's school" was to learn the names of flowers, "For how would you like it if people didn't call you by your name?" Muir had been forced to memorize the Bible and to listen to his father's extremist teachings of hell-fire and damnation, which the son could not believe. John wanted his children to love but not to fear God. Louie agreed and so their unconventional religious training was expressed in love of people, nature and animals. Wanda embodied love, as was was shown in her first literary expression. Her long chant of wonder and thanksgiving was recorded by her mother and treasured by her father. Part of it ran:

Martinez, Cal.
Oct. 15, '86.

Oh we love this world that we live in and we do not know much about any other world. Oh we love the days in this beautiful world, for we can run and play and have a grand time, and the Lord can see us all the time and we cannot see Him. Oh how grand and great He is! Oh how grand and great He is! He makes all people, all dogs, and even all hens. He makes gold and silver. How grand and great He is! He makes frogs and elephants—the lovely stars and moon, and all things. We love Him, oh we love Him! . . .

Muir Papers, Holt-Atherton Pacific Center for Western Studies

Holt-Atherton Pacific Center for Western Studies

A self-portrait by John Muir.

II

"...oh Papa, when are you coming home?"

January 23, 1886, was another red-letter day for the Muirs and Strentzels for that was the date of Helen Lillian Muir's birth. From the very first her life was in peril for she was fragile and heir to every germ.

Wanda lost her status as the only child to become the big and protective sister. Although not quite five, she had the emotional security not to be jealous of the ailing infant and continued to reign as the light and life of the anxious household.

In February, 1887, she was at her father's side while he drew a shaggy self-portrait for an old Indiana friend.

•

Wanda, peeping past my elbow, asks, "Is that you Papa?" and then goes on to say that it is just like me, only the hair is not curly enough . . . I think that you will surely like her. She remarked the other day that she was worth seeing now, having got a new gown or something that pleased her . . .

•

Once Helen seemed healthy enough so that Muir dared leave home for more than a day or two, Louie and Wanda sent him bulletins. Wanda was almost seven when she wrote her first letter "alon" to Dear Papa.

•

March 13, 1888

Dear Papa:

I hope you are well. The baby is well and sweet and we are all well the baby is sweeter every day.

Part of the time it is warm and nice and part of the time is cold when will you come home dear papa. I wort this leter all alon.
drip drip the rain is falling
chip chip the birds are calling.
the cherry blows are in bloom and the peach blows are in bloom.

The baby wrote a little letter too you. Grandma and Grandpa are well.

•

By 1887 Muir was burdened with ranch work which was not advantageous to his career. He was not writing even so much as a journal. "I am all nerve-shaken and lean as a crow—loaded with care, work and worry," he confided to one of his brothers that year. Both family and friends were relieved when he accepted editorship of the two-volume book *Picturesque California*, a job that entailed writing, supervision of other writers, and research trips. In July of 1888 he left the "humdrum, work-a-day life" to travel to Mount Shasta, Mount Rainier, and as far north as Vancouver. He was accompanied by his close friend, landscape artist William Keith. Like Muir, Keith had been born and had spent his childhood in Scotland. Together they reveled in the Scots dialect, reciting verses of Robert Burns, arguing and bantering. While Keith sketched, Muir collected material for the book and revived himself with what he termed "wilderness health." As usual, he missed his family, was concerned for them, and eager for their letters.

•

July 24, 1888

My Dear Papa:

I hope you are well. I am well. Baby is sweeter than ever and she is very well.

The weather is very warm and the musketos are bad. We are still at home. the musketos bit me very much and baby too and we had to sta up in your room most of the time.

Tomorrow will be babys birthday and we intend to eat out on the porch for fun and I think that it will be nice to do it. Grandmama stays with us a goodel of the time.

Now I will begin with a rime, I love the birds their sweet songs last until the evening comes then they go to sleep among the branches sweet.

When will you be home papa.

baby made these scribbles and blots for a letter and says she is writing to Papa. the baby went to sleep holding your picture and saying over and over "I love my dear papa I love my dear papa."

Grandpa and Grandma are well. Grandma stays with us every night since auntie went to the city.[1]

Oh Papa when are you coming home? I want to see you so very much my dear Papa.

I wish I could be with you and see those beautiful mountains. I want to kiss you papa, goodby.

Annie Wanda Muir.

Seattle, W.T. Aug. 1, 1888

My dear Wanda,

Your nice good letter came yesterday & I was very glad to get it far gladder than you know for I had not heard a word from home since I left you all; & when I got to this town I went very quick & in a very anxious frame of mind to the post office expecting to find five or six letters but there was none at all & I was very sorry for I wanted so much to hear that you & Helen & Mama & everybody were well. I had to go to a hotel & felt very sad & had a sore heart. Keith got two letters, & next day his wife came. He said, "never mind Muir everybody is well at your house & things are so smooth & regular they never thought there was anything to write about but you will get a letter soon anyway.["] Then I went again to the post office & waited a long time for my turn & asked the man in the Office if there was a letter for John Muir & spelled the name for him, M.u.i.r. but after looking over a big lot of letters he said No, & shook his head. Then I went again & again until I thought there was no use going any more But Keith said yesterday "Muir lets go to the Post Office You are sure to get a letter today" & so I went with him as I was soon going to leave Seattle & I thought I must try once more before going away into the woods and sure enough the man gave me your letter & I opened it & looked anxiously down the page until I came to the

1. Muir had brought his ill sister, Annie Muir, from Wisconsin in 1887 in hopes that California climate would restore her health. It did, and she returned home in July, 1888. In Northern California, then as now, "the city" means San Francisco.

the place where you said we are all well & I was very glad for I was afraid that Helen might be sick. Then I read all the letter & found it very interesting from beginning to end . . .

Yesterday Mr. Keith & I went on a little steamboat to Port Blakeley across the sound from here & looked at the big sawmills & walked into the woods to see the trees & the flowers & we had a good time & got back here at night. The trees are very tall, some of them about three hundred feet high & very beautiful with glossy green branches & brown cones, & beneath the trees there are many kinds of bushes. The spiraeas, two species are very handsome one with white & the other with purple flowers. The one with white flowers is very delicate & feathery & fifteen or twenty feet high. Then there is a charming little rose mixed in with them & lots of hazel bushes with nuts on them & raspberry & black berry bushes loaded with fruit & we ate lots of them & lots of huckleberry bushes with nice smooth red berries ripe now & juicy But the Salal berries are black & they are the most abundant of all. The bushes are not very high the highest only about as high as your head & most of them lean over & spread on the ground like vines. All the ground is covered with them for miles & miles. The leaves are large & firm & handsome & the flowers are pink bells. I wish you could see them Here are a few that I gathered for you but they will be all withered before you get them. Some day I will take You into these beautiful wild woods & then You will see the dear little vine that is called Linnaea. I found one flower for You. Most of the flowers have faded a month ago.

Your rhyme, or rim as you called it is very good I think & I hope you will send me some more. Tell Mama that I expected to leave this town three or four days ago, but had to wait for others to get ready. Tomorrow we go across the mtns by the Snohomish Falls then through the woods by Green River to Mt Rainier. Guess I will not be able to climb to the top of it, & the weather is not safe, but I will see some of the glaciers at least & the grand old trees.[1]

Good bye. Send Your next letters to Portland. In about 2 weeks I may be there. Give my love to everybody at both homes & take good care of little Helen.

Your loving Father

---

1. Later Muir wrote his wife, "Did not mean to climb it, but got excited and soon was on top."

Muir Papers, Holt-Atherton Pacific Center for Western Studies

Muir's beloved "bairns," Wanda and Helen, circa 1888.

August 7, 1888

My dear Papa,

I hope you are well now. I was sorry you felt sick. we are well baby looks sweeter every day and is very well. she cried a good deal at the musketos becous we would not let her play out in the garden and then she wanted mamma all the time.

Last Sunday we were planning how to go to the city and Helen lay still without talking till we were thru then she said "I dont want mama stay at any more folks" Most of the time she wont let Grandma put her to sleep but wants mamma. the musketos have come agen and they are awful.

Dear Papa your two letters reached me safely with the flowers and they were so lovely. I was sorry that the bear caught your hand.[1] How I wish I could go with you and see the lovely flowers and trees and climb the mountains and see the glaciers and drink the cold pure glacier water.

O Papa please bring me some of the bonny spireas and sweet wild roses.

did you eat meny of those nice berries? I wish I could go along and eat as many as I want. we have fine big peaches and Bartletts here, but no berries.

Those mountains must be perfectly grand, but O Papa dont climb too far if the weather is stormy.

When are you coming home dear Papa? I want to see you so much and Helen says too very often, "I want to see my own dear Papa I goin write tell him to come home and stay with baby", and she did look so sweet trying to write.

Aunt Annie reached Lincoln all right and well August 1.

I hope you will send me another letter soon, and some bonny mosses and many ferns.

Your loving little girl,

Annie Wanda Muir.

•

On the very day Muir was ascending Mount Rainier "heart and limb exultant and free," Louie wrote one of her few existing letters:

•

1. In his July 23 letter to Wanda, Muir had told her that, when he petted a chained bear, the animal had bitten his hand "a little."

A ranch that needs and takes the sacrifice of a noble life or work, ought to be flung away beyond all reach and power for harm . . . The Alaska book and the Yosemite book, dear John, must be written, and you need to be your own self, well and strong, to make them worthy of you. There is nothing that has the right to be considered beside these except the welfare of our children.

•

Her wise decision, to which he agreed, was soon implemented by the selling or leasing of much of the land and later in hiring an able ranch manager.

From 1889 on, Muir had fewer cares while the family lived on the earnings assured by his hard work on the ranch.

Early in June, 1889, he returned to Yosemite Valley with Robert Underwood Johnson, an associate editor of the *Century Magazine*, which had succeeded *Scribner's Monthly*. They were distressed and indignant over the devastation there and in Tuolumne Meadows caused by man, sheep, and cattle. " . . . money-changers were in the temple." Muir and Johnson's concern stimulated plans to make the high country surrounding the Valley, which was protected as a State Grant, into a National Park.

Their campaign was launched by the *Century*'s publication of Muir's vigorous articles against the abuse of nature. These articles were widely quoted and influential enough to get a bill introduced into Congress. They also stirred an amazing conservation drive, that, coupled with Johnson's lobbying with congressmen, culminated in the creation of Yosemite National Park on October 1, 1890. The money changers were swept from the temple!

Johnson, aged 36 in 1889, was an expansive man, well-acquainted with men of prominence, especially in the literary world. Muir's directness, humor and commitment to preservation delighted the editor. After their Yosemite trip, Johnson was unceasingly supportive of Muir in advancing the cause of protection, and seeing to it that Muir himself received recognition.[1] As editor and friend, he had tremendous impact.

Despite Muir's love of, and need for, "wanderings in the wilderness," he wrote Louie from Yosemite that "whatever mode of travel I am to do must be done soon, as it grows ever harder to leave my nest and young." Subsequent letters from young Wanda must have further divided his conflicting allegiances.

•

1. See Johnson's *Remembered Yesterdays*, Little, Brown, and Company, 1923.

June 4, 1889

My dear Papa.

We are all very well, and I hope you are well and not very tired after the long stage ride. Your telegram from Wawona came yesterday. Mama says the mountains all the way from that place are glorious. She told me about the great sugar pines and the lovely Azaleas and so many butiful caskeds.

How I wish I cood be with you today. O dear Papa when will I be strong enoufe to climb the mountains with you? Don't you think in a year or two I might?

Helen keeps asking why Papa does not come home with baby today? She is very well and is now running races with little Brownie.

We come home in the daytime but stay at Grandpa's at night. We took all your note books over to Grandpa's house.[1] This morning Mamma read about the dear little water ouzel singing in the clear cool spray. O I wish I cood see it and hear it sing. We found another little goldfinch on its nest in the rose near the tank; and it is so sweet and gentle and lets us come very near without flying off.

baby says she wants to write a little letter to dear Papa. and there are many good kisses too from baby and me.

Your loving little girl,

Annie Wanda Muir

•

Her next letter was short and to the point.

•

Martinez
July 12. 1889.

O my dear Papa do come home and see us.

Annie Wanda Muir

•

Wanda's plea reached Muir at the Grand Hotel in San Francisco where he had isolated himself in order to complete his articles for *Picturesque California*. His hotel room was a cell for work and a temporary respite from the constant interruptions of the ranch and the activities of two little girls who had difficulty keeping quiet while he worked.

While at the Grand, he wrote a friend, he could "peg away

---

1. Muir's early journals, which formed the basic text of his books, were so prized by his family that they took them with them when they stayed overnight at the Strentzels'.

Yosemite Research Library Collection

For nearly a decade, Yosemite Valley was Muir's home and haunt, and he never lost his reverence for it.

awkwardly and laboriously until the wee sma' hours or thereabouts, working long and hard and accomplishing little." After he had produced his eloquent passages, he copied them to send to Louie for her comment.

During his stay he allowed a singular diversion, an interview with a newspaper reporter. Innocently, Muir responded to questions about snakes and was later horrified to read a "villainous article" of wild reptile stories attributed to him. To Louie he wrote wryly:

Jul 4, 1889
S.F., Calif.
Grand Hotel

Hope . . . the babies are well. I feel nervous about them after reading about those geological snakes of John Muir . . .
I hope I'll survive though the Examiner makes me say 'If the poison gets into them it takes no time at all to kill them' [the hogs] & my skin is not as thick. Remember me to Grandma Grandpa & the babies & tell them not the sad story about the snakes . . .

•

His response to Wanda's letter was snake-less.

•

Grand Hotel, S.F.
July 14th, 1889

My dear Wanda

Your letter to me was very short but very delightful & charming & the illustrations at the end very original & fine. I wish I could see you tonight though you went to bed long ago & no doubt are asleep for it is now midnight, & I will see you in a day or two for my writing is nearly done.

I see very few people in my room & I speak only about three words a day to anybody though there are so many people in San Francisco. I never go out of my room except when I go to my meals. But though I am lonesome I see a good deal of myself for there are five mirrors in my room, two of them large enough to give my whole length.

Once when I was going to my dinner I saw seven little monkeys in a bird cage all huddled close together to keep warm They were the smallest monkeys I ever saw, not half as big as a cottontail rabbit and all the seven not half as big as Brownie; and yet their funny little faces were just like little old mens faces and they looked so sober & never laughed & kept winking so much I couldnt help laughing at them. Tell Helen about them. And today when I was eating my supper I saw a queer looking man. He had very long mustaches but yet he looked silly though I think he liked his mustaches better than anything else for he kept playing with them & fondling them as if they were little puppies. He looked something like this

Muir Papers, Holt-Atherton Pacific Center for Western Studies

You and Helen had better write & tell what You want me to bring You when I come home. And if you dont write very soon I will be home before your letter gets here. Tell your Mamma that though I am tired I am not so badly off as she thinks—only my head is too hot & feet too cold, thats all.

Now good night my dear & may Heaven ever bless you & keep you safely & Helen & Mamma & Grandpa & Grandma & all.

J M

August 28, 1889

My dear Papa,

I hope you are well. Helen and I are well, but Mama was sick in bed all day yesterday, so we cood not go home. We brought your notes all over to Grandpa's because Mrs. Bush had to go home and the moskeetos are just awful again, and poor little Brownie howls about them other wise he is as well as usual. Baby could not play in the garden at all.

Dear Papa why do you not write to me? It is so lonesome without you. How soon do you think that you can come home?

Poor Grandma is not well at all and she looks very pale. baby too is writing a little letter to you and she just now said "Wanda you must not shake the table when I write, it makes me dizzy."

Baby sends many kisses to you and says she is sorry that she did not kiss you when you went away.

Dear Papa good-by.

Your loving little girl

Annie Wanda Muir

•

On June 14, 1890, Muir sailed for Alaska "like a Crusader bound for the Holy Land." A winter bout with grippe had resulted in a bronchial cough and the tedium of writing had brought on nervous indigestion. A doctor warned that the trip in his weakened condition would kill him. Muir's reply was, "If I don't go I'll pay for it with my life."

Three months of explorations, peril and exhilaration, particularly on the Muir Glacier, "cured" him for "no microbe could survive in this icy world." His letters home revealed that nature once again was the best physician.

•

Victoria B.C. June 17th '90

Dear Wanda.

I told you I would be on the bounding billows when I went to Alaska & so I was. The sea was all rumpled up with big waves & the tops of them came on to the deck of the steamer & made everybody go inside of their rooms, & many were sick on account of pitching & heaving & rocking of the ship. But I was used to it & enjoyed it. & the waves were very blue at the bottom & green in the middle & white at the top. At one place off Crescent City there are many strange looking rocks, & it was a grand sight to see the huge waves dash against them & jump up more than a hundred feet in the air in pure white foam, thick & broad & massy, wilder far & more beautiful than the Yosemite waterfalls.

That was on Sunday & the wind was so strong that the sailors called it a "gale." I often thought of you when the sea was so beautiful & wild & wished you could be with me to see it. Some day you will I hope. You must write to me at Glacier Bay Alaska.

Goodbye

[John Muir]

My dear Papa.

I doo hope you are well. I have been very well since you saw me last, but Mama and Helen had awful colds, they are well now,

Three generations of Strentzels, Muirs, and Hannas lived in this still-existent Alhambra Valley home.

Courtesy of Sherry Hanna

except Mama has the toothake. Grandpa and Grandma are very happy to have us here. they both look much better now. We drove over to our own home this morning everything looked very pleasant. the windmill is mended and the tank is full of nice water. Mr. Coe says "they have pancakes every day and they are good ones too and plenty of fried rabbits."

None of the Chinamen wanted to chop wood and all went off to the city except Jimmie King and Choy. We took a box of nice ripe peaches next the fig tree. The little chikens are all rite, and yesterday 8 more little chikens came out from the pampas grass, they are all black. The wind blew just awfully for several days, but Jimmie says the grapevines are "all lite, heap good."

Mama is so scared about the diphtheria that she does not let us go near Martinez . . . [1]

I want you to come home as soon as you can. Papa, I am very lonesome without you. I wonder if you saw the moon and the planet Venus night before last, they shone so bright and looked nearly touching each other in the sky.

Yesterday the census man came here and asked us how old we were and how much land we had and what our names were and many other things . . .

Little Fido behaves very well since he came over here and is much braver, he stands up on the steps and barks at all the strange men and dogs, just as if he felt big enough to take care of all this big house.

Dear Papa when do you think that you can come home? it seems a long time since you went away.

Baby is writing you a little letter too, and asks Mama if you can read that kind of writing and we think that you can.

Please write to me soon my dear Papa. Good night.

Your loving little girl,

Annie Wanda Muir

[Dear Wanda,][2]

. . . & I climbed another mountain and a beautiful bird like a hen only far prettier, called a ptarmigan, let me close up to it and

1. Mrs. Muir's only brother had died at the age of nine from diphtheria, and as a result the family had an overwhelming dread of the disease.
2. Fragment of letter written about July 15, 1890.

feet with feathers down to its toes to keep them warm in the snow in winter. & the ground in some places was just covered with flowers like a fine garden. & I saw a humming bird, & I wondered how the little fellow found his way over the ice so far to these flowers. I will be glad to get home, so that I can see my little girls. & now here is a picture of my sled, for I think you never saw a sled. It has no wheels like wagons or buggies, but just slides. It was just wonderful how it could jump over rough places if you pulled it hard.

When I come I will tell you many fine long good stories about things. Write me another letter, & your loving Papa will be glad.

[John Muir]

Martinez, California
July 19, 1890

My dear dear Papa:

I do hope you are well now, and your throat does not hurt any more, and that the sun is still shining bright and that you had a glorious Fourth of July. The beautiful letters you wrote to us came day before yesterday, and O how glad we all were to hear from you. It seemed such a long time since your letter from Victoria.

Oh Papa how I wish I could be with you to see that great blue Glacier, and the lovely colors of the icebergs, but not to stay too long in any cold wind and fog.

The dear little flowers you sent me are so lovely. Papa, how strange it must be to see them growing close by the ice. Maybe you can find some ripe seeds of that beautiful Epilobium [fireweed] to bring when you come.[1]

Helen said this morning, "I do not want to climb any Glaciers, they are too cold. I just want my Papa to come home and stay with me." We are so glad that party of men are going to camp near you, it will not be so lonesome. Helen is well now, but had toothake in the night and Dr. Moore came and pulled it out. She cried, but we had a nice little maltese kitten here to quiet her, and it is very pretty and Mama almost likes it. Our own cat is well and has got gentle so Helen and I can cach him when we want to, but when Mama comes near, he runs away. Carlo and I were playing near the apple tree, and a big rat looked out from the vines. I said, "sikem," and Carlo jumped and caught it . . .

I have six little fishes and four polywogs in a bowl for pets, and they are just as cunning as can be. One of the polywogs has 4 feat and climbs out of the water on my finger.

The Bees are here yet.

The days are very warm here now. The North wind blew today and brought some bad mosquitos and they are trying to come in thru the window.

Grandpa and Grandma are not very well. They seem so tired every day, but they are glad to have us here and want us to stay all the time.

Dear Papa I want you to come home, and so does Helen. Mama wants you to come home very very much.

Good bye,

Your loving little girl

Annie Wanda Muir

•

October, 1890, marked the beginning of a new era for John Muir and his family. His role as a leader in preservation battles was established once Yosemite, Sequoia and General Grant National Parks were created that month. His name and authority were nationally known, and his writing was in demand.

On October 31 John T. Strentzel died. He was buried in the family plot in Alhambra Valley which his descendants still maintain. Soon after his father-in-law's death, Muir wrote, "The family is broken like a house torn asunder and half taken away." That loss necessitated the Muirs' move to the "Big House" so Grandma Strentzel could have family care and companionship. Within a few months their old house was occupied by Muir's sister, Maggie, and her farmer husband, John Reid, who had moved from Wisconsin. As planned, Reid became the ranch foreman, which relieved Muir of many responsibilities. At last he had more freedom to travel, to write, and to fight for the preservation of trees and mountains.

Living in the "Big House" was strange at first for it was not as compact and homey as the Muirs' old home. Downstairs there were large, high-ceilinged rooms, individually equipped with small marble fireplaces. The east parlor was turned into a bed-sitting room for Mrs. Strentzel. Dr. Strentzel's rather dark redwood-paneled office and library seemed to be the natural place for Muir to work. Instead he established his "scribble den" in the light-filled northwest upstairs bedroom, away from the confusion and noise of the household. From one window he could see the Carquinez Strait and Suisun Bay.

The big house was an exciting place for the two little girls, for it had innumerable hiding places. There was the big cupola bell tower at

Courtesy of Sherry Hanna

John T. Strentzel (1813-1890), a Polish exile, achieved success as both a California physician and horticulturist.

the top, a huge attic that housed intriguing relics, such as some of Muir's early inventions, and a spacious cellar.

Muir's importance brought many visitors to the house for meetings, meals, and overnight stays. A few stayed for weeks, and occasionally a relative would remain for a year or more. Formal entertainment was rare, yet hospitality was unbounded. Muir had a reputation as a thrifty Scotsman, but his generosity to his family and friends was constant. One intimate of the home was "Willie" Keith whose visits were welcomed by all. Mrs. Strentzel suggested subjects for him to paint. Muir enjoyed bantering with his fellow Scot, and the girls loved the hilarious romps over the encircling hills with the two men.

After his writing work, Muir would walk, tell droll stories, and play with his beloved daughters. As Wanda said, "Father was the biggest, jolliest child of us all."

"Wherever a Scotsman goes, there goes Burns," Muir said, as he recited verses on their rambles. Lessons in botany were part of the walks for not even a tiny bloom escaped his eyes. "See this darling little muggins?" He would kneel beside it, and launch into a loving description. They saw hillsides blue with brodiaea or larkspur, a rocky slope bright with red Indian paint brush, or an open glade knee-deep in buttercups. They knew cool, damp dells under the laurels where maidenhair ferns grew beside a little spring. They loved the buckeye balls that were just sprouting, and acorns that had lain in the damp leaf mold until life was stirring within. Muir named one hill in Alhambra Valley Mount Wanda, and another Mount Helen. It is no wonder that his daughters missed him sorely, even when he was as close as San Francisco.

He was so easily distracted and sensitive to noise that his wife and daughters almost whispered and tiptoed when he was making "booksellers bricks" in his study. Writing was never easy for him, and the tension of it often made him short-tempered and irritable. Louie, who loved music, never played her piano when he was at home, and the girls practiced their music lessons in a soundproof room over the kitchen. At times, however, he fled by train to the masculine domain of the University Club in San Francisco or a hotel and holed up until he completed his project. He kept in touch with Martinez by mail rather than telephone, as he found that the new-fangled gadget was inadequate for anything other than a shouting match.

•

University Club
San Francisco
Feb. 11, 1892

My dear Wanda,

I got your nice letter this morning, & Helen's. I wrote to Helen last night. I am very sorry Mamma is unwell & hope she will soon be better. Tell her to keep out of that windy gusty kitchen as much as possible. I dont cough at all now. I'll be home on the 4 o'clock train Saturday & will try to stay a week, & then we will not be so lonesome.

I am glad to hear Grandma is better.

Helen, my dear, I dont know when Mr Keith is coming to see you. He is quite well & is painting a great many fine pictures. Some day you & Wanda must make a visit to the city & see all the pictures in the studio. Mr Keith would be very glad then, so glad he would not know how to behave. I'll ask him next time I see him when he is going to make you another visit, & will not forget the Chocolate.

Give my love to Mamma & Grandma & Miss Graydon & study your lessons & be good I was going to say, but no use saying that for you are always good & always will be.[1] Goodbye my dear till Saturday.

Your loving papa John Muir.

•

In the spring of 1892, a family crisis summoned Muir to Portage, Wisconsin. Brother David's firm of Parry and Muir had gone bankrupt because of Parry's poor land investments, and creditors were hounding David and his wife, Juilette. John's presence and national prestige aided David. Generously, John and Louie offered him a portion of their ranch on a share-the-profits arrangement. David accepted, and he and the land prospered. Eventually, he was able to repay his debts.

While in Portage, John Muir cheered the family and insisted they appear normally at church and in town. His own depression showed only in letters home.

•

1. As a child, Katherine Merrill Graydon had been among the friends who had comforted Muir during his convalescence from the eye injury. Her 1892 visit to his home was a "great blessing," he said. After she tutored the Muir girls for several months, he helped her secure a teaching job in the Oakland High School under his friend, J. B. McChesney. ("Personal Recollections of John Muir," by Samuel Merrill, Sierra Club *Bulletin*, XIII.)

Portage Wis. Apr. 18, 1892

My dear Wanda

The people here who have heard so much about you all keep asking why did you not bring Wanda? She is old enough to travel & just think what a joy it would be to Grandma Muir to see her at least once. I have been feeling stupid & headachy since coming here. Yesterday I went to church with Mother, & many of the old acquaintances came up & spoke to me.

This country seems cold & flat compared with Cal. I'll tell you about the places & things I saw when I get home. How you would enjoy Joannas children. Remember me to Miss Graydon. Your loving papa

John Muir

Martinez, Cal.
April 18, 1892

My dear Papa:

When are you coming home?

I hope it will be soon for it seems as if it was a long time since you were here.

I hope you are well and that you had a pleasant Easter.

I will be very glad indeed to have a letter from you, for we have not heard yet.

I am learning a little piece [by Robert Burns] which begins, "Wee, modest, crimson-tipped flower, Thou's met me in an evil hour"; and which I think is pretty. Do you like it?

. . . Cousin Anna and Jessie expect to start home next week.

Miss Graydon, Helen and I went over to the other place and had a pleasant little visit.

I can not write a long letter because Mama is ready to start to Martinez.

With much love,

Wanda

•

May 28, 1892, was an historic day for John Muir. After months of talk and planning with mountaineering friends, they completed organization of the Sierra Club. The formal purpose was, "To explore, enjoy and render accessible the mountain regions of the Pacific Coast; to publish authentic information concerning them; to enlist the support and cooperation of the people and the government in preserving the forests and other natural features of the Sierra Nevada Mountains." Muir described it far less formally when he said the men were "hoping that we will be able to do something for wildness and make the mountains glad."

At home that night, he was excited and jubilant. Until then he had been a voice in the wilderness for the wilderness. Now a host of like-minded people would support him. Incorporation took place June 4, 1892. John Muir was elected president, a position he held until his death. He and "Muir, Miss Wanda, Martinez" were listed among the charter members.[1]

•

University Club
San Francisco
April 30, 1893.

My dear Helen and Wanda

I received your nice letters & I was very glad to hear you were all well & to get the little cedar sprays.

You must not be too lonesome. I'll soon be home & I'm not far away anyhow. I suppose I could hear your sweet voices in the telephone, but not very well I fear. I couldnt hear Mamma the other day, nor Mr Borland either very well, so I got only part of the message. Tell Mama next time to telegraph or write. Also, tell her that I will be home Wednesday morning & perhaps Mr and Mrs Myrick may come with me.[2] If they do I will telegraph as soon as I know.

I'm getting on pretty well but slowly & I dont sleep much.

Keith had a grand reception of which he is very proud. The Sierra Club meeting was also a grand success.

Love to you my dear babies & to Mamma & Grandma.

from your affectionate father

John Muir

•

Until then, Muir's travels had been confined to the western states and Alaska, but in 1893 he and Keith decided to stop talking about Scotland and go to Europe together. Keith started first after writing Muir in May, "I can't wait any longer. I'm starting tomorrow."

There followed a cross-country chase with Muir always one telegram behind. The World's Columbian Exposition in Chicago was to

1. Her initial membership lasted only one year. She rejoined on her own in 1905 and remained a member until December 1929.
2. M. H. Myrick, a charter member of the Sierra Club.

be their meeting place. Muir arrived to find Keith's message, "Couldn't stand the crowd. Will wait in New York."

Muir viewed the Exposition, then boarded a train for New York.

•

Chicago, May 26 1893

My dear Wanda

I was very very glad to get your letter at Portage, It was there waiting for me when I got to Grandma Muirs house. I let Joanna & Sarah & Annie & all of them read it & they said what a good letter it was & how glad they would have been if you had been with me. I told them that both you & Helen would soon be old enough to travel & then you would come & see them. Grandma Muir is quite well & does not seem to change much though she is eighty years old. Annie is about the same as when she was in California & Joanna's little girls are very sweet & good especially Bessie. They stayed out of school & followed me all over town the day I was there.

Tell Mama I called on Mr. Rodgers, & he & many others asked kindly for Uncle David & Aunt Ette.[1]

Ette's father & mother came to see me in the evening & asked all about her & David & wished they were not too old to go to California. I also called on Ette's brother & he seemed anxious to go to California. Also on Ette's brother-in-law who is just determined to sell out & go to raise grapes & peaches etc.

The fair is very big some of the buildings would reach all the way across Alhambra Valley & half way up Franklin Canon for all I know.[2] But the show of canned peaches, crockery, buggies, stuffed owls and things dont interest me so very much. The whole show is nothing to my own two sweet babies. With much love, my dear Wanda & Helen—All I have. I am

Your loving papa

John Muir

•

This was Muir's first trip east since youth and editor Johnson saw to it that he met peers, attended luncheons and dinners, and visited Walden Pond as well as Emerson's home and gravesite. Botanist Charles Sargent, paleontologist Henry Fairfield Osborn and others were entertained by the Scotsman's stories, and impressed by his

1. By then, David and Juliette Muir had resettled in Martinez.
2. Franklin Canyon adjoined the Strentzel-Muir property on the west.

intelligence, integrity and modesty. In turn, Muir was delighted with his new friends, though bemused by the social whirl and the heat.

•

Martinez, Cal.
June 2, 1893

My dear Papa:

We received your three letters from Chicago also your telegram from New York. How long do you expect to stay in N.Y.?

Mama says she thinks you must be having a fine time with all those fine people.

How do you like John Burroughs?[1] Will you have time to sail up the Hudson River?

I suppose Mr. and Mrs. Keith have enjoyed the trip too, but they must have been in a great hurry at Chicago.

Helen has been very well all the time and we all have, with the exception that Mama's eyes trouble her very much.

O Papa it is so lonesome here with out you, and Helen keeps asking how soon we think that you can come home. I hope the weather has been as delightful where you have been as it is here. But today it is very warm and the cherries are ripening fast.

We have had a good deal of trouble with Mr. Hefner's dogs. They came up around the house and they chased May and scared her awfully but the Chinamen drove them off before they got very close to her.[2] When any body goes near them or throws clods at them they growl. Mr. Coleman went over and talked to Mr. Hefner and he promised to keep them shut up un till he can sell them.

Aunt Margaret has been pretty well all the time lately. We went to Uncle David's yesterday and everything looks nice there and the bing cherries are delicious and the May dukes are nearly ripe.

The mosquitoes were dreadful though along the hedge and I am afraid they will come here and keep us in the house.

Just now Elfie came along and jumped up in my lap and sniffed over the paper as if to see what I could be doing and then ran away to play with Helen.

---

1. From their first meeting on June 1, 1893, writer-naturalist "John o' the birds" Burroughs and John "o' the mountains" Muir were argumentative, competitive friends.

2. Margaret and John Reid's daughter, May, and her husband Arthur Coleman aided Louie when Muir was away. Muir made Coleman his business manager.

Mama is trying to teach me to sing and I have learned three tunes.
I gave one of my canarys to Emily Hayward.
Where shall we direct our next letters to you?
Do you think you will come back by way of Chicago as you stayed such a short time there?
Now dear Papa do take good care of your self, and try not to go in any dangerous places.
Please write to me soon, for the time is so long waiting to hear from you.

Your loving daughter,

Wanda Muir.

New York, June 7, 1893

My dear Wanda,

. . . It has been very hot here & I felt all the time as if somebody had rubbed the inside of my underclothes with very sticky molasses. The papers said that the day before yesterday was the hottest 5th of June ever known in New York. Yesterday was also very horribly hot, but I did not feel it much for Mr Johnson took me up the Hudson river to one of the beautiful residences, Mr Osborne's in the Hudson Highlands, where we dined & drank cool water & champagne & drove about the leafy woods & gathered purple lady slippers & trailing arbutus & sailed on the charming river.[1] Mr Johnson has kept me wining & dining & seeing people at the clubs so I have not been able to write much. This afternoon he is going to take me to Boston & Cambridge to see Sargent & the University people to talk about the forests. This trip will take two days.[2]

Tell Mama that the Century people are going to print my first book instead of Appletons, & promise to make a better portrait of me, as they say that the one in the Magazine was not good, not half handsome enough.[3]

Mr Keith has been in a fussy hurry ever since we started & left for

1. Henry Fairfield Osborn, 1857-1935, was president of the American Museum of Natural History and his estate reflects his botanical interest. He and Muir became close friends.

2. Charles Sprague Sargent, Harvard botanist and first director of the Arnold Arboretum in Boston.

3. Muir's first book, *The Mountains of California*, published by the Century Company in 1894, was a revised compilation of his essays on the Sierra Nevada which had been published in magazines.

Glasgow nearly a week ago & I fear I will not see much of him.

I think I will not get away from here for a week or more yet: But I feel well, & will take so many letters to people in Europe that I may not miss Keith so much.

Everybody I meet here tries to make me feel at home & seems determined to keep me talking about the mountains & woods & glaciers I have seen & loved & studied so long. I think I am getting a little fatter eating so much new stuff the names of which I dont know. Tell Mama that I heard somebody say yesterday that strawberries are bad for rheumatism.

I hope you are all well & that you take good care of little darling Helen. I showed Mrs Osborne your pictures yesterday, the lady who entertained us in the Highlands at "Castle Crag" & she said you both looked like poets.

Love to all

John Muir

Martinez, California
June 12, 1893

My dear Papa,

I suppose that you will have crossed the bounding billows by the time this letter reaches you. I hope that there has been no storms while you are on the waters and that you will be well. We are all very well here but Grandma. She has been real sick and has been in bed several days but she is a little better today. Helen is very well and she is getting heavy. She weighs 48 pounds.

I hope that Mr. John Burrows will go with you to Scotland as I think it would be much pleasenter than for you to go alone.

How is Mr. and Mrs. Keith and where does she expect to stop while you and Mr. Keith are climbing mountains? You must have had a fine time on the Hudson river. I wish I had been along.

We have taken Elfie in to our rooms at night and she approves greatly and so do I. She sleeps in a box in the fire place.

The cherries are very nearly gone. We have had some nice ones. Have you had any good ones where you have been?

The boat and tusks and things were sent. Mr. Coleman took them down on the boat and saw that they got there all right.

We had three very warm days where the thommenter went up to 98 but since then it has been very cool but the mosketos have been very bad sometimes . . .

With love and kisses from us all I close.

Wanda

New York, June 14, 1893
10.20 A.M.

My dear Wanda.

When I got back from Boston yesterday morning, I made haste to the Century Rooms to see if any letters had come from home & I was very glad to find one from you, a good long one telling just what I wanted to know, that you were all well . . . I got a good view of all at home as if I had been there myself. And this shows your letter was a very good one.

I'm glad you are learning to sing, for everything in the world sings in some way or other. Even the mosquitoes along the hedge, & the sand under your feet, as well as the birds & winds & streams & I had almost said pianos.[1] . . .

I suppose the May-dukes & peaches will soon be ripe & then you will all have a good-time making and breaking those things you call "cobblers."

You may tell Mama and Grandma that I was at another champagne supper last night, & I am to go to another tonight, but my stomach seems happy & behaves like a gentleman through it all, though neither me nor my stomach knows the names or compositions of the dishes we encounter.

(bad grammar this last sentence)
(See if you or Lou can correct it.)
(I'm sure you couldn't correct the cooking.) . . .

I wrote a long letter to Mama yesterday but forgot to tell her that when we were in Cambridge we went to Col. Higginsons home & after a long pleasant talk he took us to the homes of Lowell & Longfellow.[2] Both of these are just as they were when their famous owners were living in them & Mr. Higginson knew them & made our visit very interesting. Mr. Higginson is the man who wrote the pretty out-door book I gave to Lou.

---

1. Muir had disliked piano music ever since his winters with the John Swett family in San Francisco when his writing in their attic was disturbed by the children's daily piano practice.

2. Thomas Wentworth Higginson, 1823-1911, was a writer, abolitionist, and social reformer who had guided Helen Hunt Jackson and Emily Dickinson during their early writings.

Tell Helen that I will send her pictures of Emerson & Thoreau today, & write a letter for her own dear little self tomorrow.

It has been very hot but I have stood it quite well, for Johnson took me away when it was hottest.

I must now go to work at my M.S. Ask Mama to read you the story of the ministers dog & see what you think of it.[1] Everybody here seems to think it wonderful. It is to form a separate article in the Century. Tell Mama she will find it in a book copied from the original notes. Tell Mama to keep in the shade & not read while her eyes are weak.

I shall get all your letters sent c/of the Century wherever I am. I will send my European address as soon as I know it.

Goodbye darling babies,

Your loving Papa

John Muir

Martinez, Cal.
June 15, 1893

My dear Papa:

You must have had a lovely trip on the Hudson river with Mr. Johnson. How I wish I could have been there to see the clear beautiful water and those fine homes and gardens. Oh to walk in the woods and gather ferns and the bonnie sweet Mayflowers!

Helen talks every day about the time when she will be well and strong and big enough to go traveling with you and then we could all be happy together. She begs Mama to take her to the City and says "I just know that I will not get sick this time."

You speak of the weather being so warm it seems only a week or so ago that they were having snow and blizzards in New York.

Yesterday Helen and I were invited to Elsie Ames' birthday party. We had a delightful time, there was a table set out under some big live oak trees. This also was delightful and so were the strawberries on it. Judge Ames has a lovely place.

Grandma is able to sit up and to go around the house. Aunt Margaret and May come over quite often, they were all well the last time I saw them.

1. "Stickeen" was the dog who had won Muir's heart and pen during an 1881 Alaskan trip. Muir's frequently told story of this dog was published in 1897.

Helen's chickens and turkeys are growing fast but they are still very gentle.

Now good by Papa and take good care of your self.

Your loving daughter

Wanda Muir

New York, June 20, 1893

Dear Wanda

I got your nice letter yesterday. I was feeling very lonesome not getting any letters from home for so long. I suppose you will say that you thought I would be away, & that therefore it would be no use to write. But I think I told you all that it would not matter whether I was away because Mr Johnson would forward them wherever I went.

It has been & is very hot here & I always feel anxious about Helen in hot weather, especially when the fruit is ripe, & might make her sick or cause toothache, So you may know I was very glad to know that she was well, & all of you & glad to hear that Grandma is better. In this hot weather she ought not to go about so much. It is ten o'clock at night here just now and the temperature is 90°, and it was 98° at 3 o'clock & damp chokey & sultry. Still I stand it pretty well, as well as the New York people. Everybody that can afford it has gone away. I will soon be cool enough for next Saturday at noon I will sail for Liverpool on the Etruria. I thought of going on the Adriatic which sails tomorrow, but I found that I will get to Liverpool as soon on Etruria though she starts three days later. She sails so much faster. I don't know where Mr Keith is. He went away two weeks ago. Maybe I'll meet him in Scotland[1] . . .

I'm glad you took in Elfie. That was sensible. I told you to do that long ago. I dont mean to go in dangerous places, & I'm going to hurry back as soon as I can. Here is a picture of Walden Pond that I think is pretty good, & I think you should keep it. Beautiful trees & flowers grow there & the water is clear, & all the banks are shady & leafy. Someday you & Mama & Helen will go there, & see

1. Twice Muir missed Keith by a day in Paris. That may have been for the better since, as Linnie Marsh Wolfe surmised, "art galleries and glaciers did not auger well for harmony." Later a humorous column entitled, "Traveling Companions. How William Keith and John Muir Did Europe Together Without Meeting," appeared in the San Francisco *Call*.

where Thoreau lived & Emerson. So much greener & fresher & calmer than Martinez is, & so many good & great people lived there. The Elm trees in particular are large & graceful. But it must be pretty cold & dreary in wintertime. Be sure to tell Helen not to eat sour cherries. You must take good care of your little sister when I am away.

I have fine letters of introduction to people in Europe & I suppose I will soon feel at home.

The ship I am going to sail on is a very fine one. So you need not be afraid of storms. My! How hot it is. Both my coat & vest are off & yet the perspiration flowing as if I were made of snow.

Give my love to Mama & Grandma & many kisses to Midge [Helen]. I wonder what I can bring you folks when I come home. I must get something nice. Remember me to Dave & Ette & Maggie & May & all the Reids. I suppose Maggie & May miss me very much & so does Lou if she is still at the ranch, for they have nobody now to tease them poor things. Tell May & Lou only servant girls broil their hair in N.Y. I tease Mr Johnson a good deal, but he teases back.

Now good night my dear Wanda. Tell Helen & Mama I'll write soon.

Martinez, Cal.
July 7, 1893

My dear Papa:

I hope that you enjoyed the voyage and that you are safe in a beautiful part of the land beyond the sea. We read in the papers that the ETRURIA reached England on the first of July.

How did you spend the glorious Fourth? We had a perfectly grand time here.

Mr. Coleman bought a lot of sky rockets, Roman candles and lots and lots of fire crackers, and he and Johnie Reid shot off the rockets. Lou, Francie and May fired the Roman candles. Uncle David and Aunt Ette were here too. Helen enjoyed it all wonderfully and was not the least bit scared or nervous. Mama wrapped her in a big shawl and she stayed with Uncle David on the porch. Aunt Margaret was too nervous to come but she feels better now.[1]

1. Margaret and Sarah Muir were semi-invalids all their lives as a result of the strenuous labor their father forced them to do in Wisconsin. John's health was also undermined by the toil, inadequate food and near-suffocation in a well he was digging.

. . . I have begun to study in good earnest and have regular hours. I am learning the Bible verses. Helen and Lou are studying also.

Elfie is as lively as ever but would not look at the fire works and ran off up stairs . . .

How do you like the country that you are in now, and how does it look?

Now take good care of your self Papa. Please write to me again soon.

From your own ever loveing daughter.

Wanda Muir

Dunbar, Scotland
July 13, 1893

Dear Wanda,

It is about 10 o'clock in the forenoon here but no doubt you are still asleep for it is about midnight at Martinez, and sometimes when it is today here it is yesterday in California on account of being on opposite sides of the round world. But ones thoughts travel fast & I seem to be in California whenever I think of you & Helen. I suppose you are busy with your lessons & peaches, peaches especially. You are now a big girl almost a woman, & you must mind your lessons & get in a good store of the best words of the best people while your memory is retentive & then you will go through the world rich.

Ask mother to give you lessons to commit to memory every day. Mostly the sayings of Christ in the gospels, & selections from the poets. Find the hymn of praise in Paradise Lost—"These are thy glorious works Parent of Good *[sic]* Almighty," and learn it well.

Last evening after writing to Helen I took a walk with Maggie Lunam along the shore on the rocks where I played when a boy.[1] The waves made a grand show breaking in sheets & sheaves of foam, & grand songs, the same old songs they sang to me in my childhood & I seemed a boy again & all the long eventful years in America were forgotten while I was filled with that glorious ocean psalm.

Tell Maggie I'm going today to see Miss Jaffry the minister's daughter who went to school with us.

1. "Maggie" was the daughter of Muir's cousin, Margaret Hay Lunam, his host. He was so moved by the poverty in Dunbar that he sent a yearly check for $100.00, half for the Lunams, half to the poor, from 1893 until his death.

& tell mama that the girl Agnes Burns that could outrun me married a minister & is now a widow living near Prestonpans. I may see her. Goodbye dear. Give my love to Grandma & everybody.

Your loving father

John Muir

Martinez, California
August 4, 1893

My dear Papa:

We have received your three beautiful letters, and Oh how very, very glad we were to get them and to see the bonny little flowers that were in them.

I wish I could be with you and see all the things you tell of in your letters. It must be so delightful to be out in the rosy Heather and to feel that you are really back in your own native land once more.

We are all well here, that is of course with the exception that Grandma is never very well, and Mama's eyes are troubling her a good deal yet.

Miss Edith Blaisdell is teaching Helen, Lou, and my self. We are all delighted with her. She has just come from the Normal school and has received a teachers certificate so that she is looking for a school, but she will stay here and teach us until she gets one.

Helen says that she just loves to study because she is so gentle with her.

Well what do you think? I saw in Saturdays paper that Mr. Keith had returned to Chicago. It said "Mr. Keith sauntered into the California Building minus John Muir. This is the way that he walked over Scotland." I will enclose the notice of his return.

I am learning to sing the "Blue Bells of Scotland."

I analyze a plant or two nearly every morning and I enjoy it so much. I also learn some verses in the Bible and read some poetry every day. I do enjoy my Botany so much. I have analyzed a good many plants but it is hard to get them for the hills are so dry.

There are some nice ripe peaches but the pears are not ripe enough to eat although they are shipping them up North.

You say that the people listen with wonder at the tales of California, but no wonder they do for of course it seems just the same to them as it does to us if you talk of Scotland or Norway.

Helen says she wants her "own dear Papa to come home." She was saying she did so want the grape time to come. I asked her what she wanted the grape time to come for when she had peaches and pears and she said "Why don't you know why? Papa is coming home then."

Before this letter reaches you you will have received a sweet little letter from Helen. I think it is very well written for a little girl her age. Every word of it is her own.

The little trees that you brought from Vancouver are growing better than they ever have before. They are getting to be quite big trees.

Hoping you will soon be home and that you are well and enjoying yourself. I remain ever your affectionate daughter

Wanda Muir

Hotel Belvedere
St. Moritz Engadino . . . Switzerland, August 25, 1893.

I think I wrote to Mama & Helen from Chamoux which I suppose you know is in France. From there I went through grand scenery to Geneva,—a beautiful town on a beautiful lake surrounded with vineyards & charming homes. Thence I went to Neufehatel another beautiful & quaint old town on the shore of a lovely lake more than 20 miles long. Here the great & famous Louis Agassiz was once a professor before he went to America.[1] Next day I went across the famous Jura Mountains through many wild gorges & tunnels to Basle, a big town on the famous river Rhine. Thence to Zurick, the most beautiful I think of all the towns of Switzerland, & the Lake of Zurick is also more beautiful than I can tell—such lovely pale blue glacier water—such picturesque shores—such grand icy mountains in the distance . . .

Today I came here in a diligence from Chinanna, another wonderful days ride through chestnut groves, vineyards, wild forests of larch & spruce, grand mountains, & O dear I dont know all what, but I'm sleepy & tired & it is late & I ought to be in bed, for I have to get up tomorrow morning about 4 o'clock to take the stage for a place called Davos or Dorfz over another pass etc.

1. Oddly, scientist Alexander Emanuel Agassiz, 1835-1910, had been born in Neufehatel, and naturalist-geologist Louis Agassiz, 1807-1873, had taught in the town's university. Although Muir never met Louis Agassiz, he was his disciple in glaciation, and Agassiz felt Muir " . . . the first man who has any adequate conception of glacial action."

Then Ill try to get to Lake Constance & the falls of the Rhine at Schafausen & then to Basle & straight back to London thence a day or two in Scotland—Ho for America & Martinez.

And now Wanda if ever you mean to travel hereabouts learn to speak french. My what a mess I make of it. Even the dogs don't understand it as I speak it & refuse to wag their tails to my "bon chien bon chien" Not one person in ten thousand understands English & when I try Chinook or pidgeon English it does no good.

I must go to bed. Good night. Good night. Good night. Love my dear Wanda to you all many kisses for Helen. Tell Mama Ill write in a day or two.

Martinez, Cal.
September 5, 1893

My dear Papa:

We have received your letters from Switzerland, and how glad we were to get them and how we enjoyed them. I wish I could have been there too and seen it all.

All are very well here. Helen in particular is very well and is enjoying the grapes.

I hope you will soon be home, how long do you think it will be before you are here. You said you would be home about grape time and the sweet waters and a few other kinds are ripe now.

The little spray of Edelweiss you sent in your last letter to Mama was beautiful. How I wish I could have a growing plant of it here at home.

Helen is still delighted with her studies. She does not tire of them as we thought she would; often she does not want to stop when school hours are over but wants to keep on studying.

We have given up going to Pacific Grove as people that have just come from there say the weather is very cold and foggy and besides Aunt Margaret concluded she was not able to go with us.

Uncle David and Aunt Ette were here last Sunday.

I am still learning 4 or 5 verses in the Bible every day and also a verse or two of poetry.

Now Papa good-by, take good care of your self and come home before long.

With love from all of us

Wanda Muir

P.S. Since I wrote this letter we received one from you saying that you had such a cold. Try not to get it any worse.

•

Even after his return to England, Muir prolonged his travels for sightseeing in London with Sir Joseph Hooker, another visit with publisher David Douglas in Edinburgh, and a last nostalgic look at Dunbar. A telegram from Louie awaited him in New York, advising him to postpone his homecoming for a side trip to Washington to influence Hoke Smith, the new Secretary of the Interior. Muir's influential talks on forest preservation with Smith and other politicians marked his first face-to-face lobbying in the nation's capital.

•

New York, Sep. 26, 1893

Dear Wanda and Helen:

I was very glad to get your letters yesterday. They were both very interesting and well written. Tell Mama that I got her telegram yesterday (Monday) but Grandma's I got Saturday. If Mr. Gilder gets back to New York tomorrow then Mr. Johnson and I will go to Washington about the forests, but I don't want to go alone.[1] This is the only thing that keeps me in New York. I mean to stay a day or two at Chicago, and with Mother, then, my dears, I'm coming straight home, declining all other invitations.

I got some clothes made in Edinburgh just before I left, and while trying them on I stood between two mirrors and saw the back of my head for the first time. Then I noticed a spot nearly bald and thought perhaps I would have to wear a wig some day and you would all be talking about it. Here is what I thought you would be saying. I hope it will amuse you a little while you are waiting for me to appear.

John Muir

Martinez, California
Sept. 26, 1893

Dear Papa:

Now you will soon be here and oh how glad we all are to think that you will really be at home in a few days. It is just delightful to think of.

I suppose that this letter will get to Portage before you do but I'll write any way and be sure of it.

Mama is having the house painted but it will be dry before you get

---

1. Richard Watson Gilder was editor-in-chief of *Century* Magazine until his death in 1909. His associate, Robert Underwood Johnson, succeeded him.

here, they are painting it a light soft grey and I think it will look very pretty . . .

I will write to Aunt Annie tomorrow morning and Helen and Mama will write to you soon.

The grapes are delicious and the prices a little better than they were.

We had a rain here a few weeks ago which makes it beautiful to walk and Miss Blaisdell goes with us often but the roads are as dusty as ever again.

Helen is planning a great many nice walks to take with you when you get home.

With much love your daughter

Wanda Muir

•

Grapes were still being picked when Muir finally arrived home early in October. He was weary but soon settled down to his "scribble den" to pick words, write six new chapters and revise and coordinate his early mountain essays into book form. As usual his wife acted as a red pencil and he sought and followed her advice. By the following April he was tired of writing as he confided to editor Johnson.

•

Apr. 3, 1894

. . . the book, begotten Heaven knows when is finished & out of me, therefore hurra etc. & thanks to you, very friend, for benevolent prodding. Six of the sixteen chapters are new, & the others are nearly so, for I have worked hard on every one of them, leaning them against each other, adding lots of new stuff, & killing adjectives & adverbs of redundant growth—the verys, intenses, gloriouses, & buts—by the score.

•

The Mountains of California was published that fall and met acclaim. At fifty-four, his first book was a success! Muir remarked this in a note to his old friend, Jeanne Carr.

•

I take pleasure in sending you with this a copy of my first book. You will say that I should [have] written it long ago; but I begrudged the time of my young mountain-climbing days.

•

He gave many copies to friends and relatives. His Dunbar cousin, Margaret Lunam, suggested that he add some personal experiences to his narratives. His reply was characteristically modest: "As to putting more of myself in these sketches, I never had the heart to spoil their symmetry with mere personal trials and adventures. It looks too much like saying, 'Here is the Lord and here is me.' Still I know very well that narrative adventures, etc. are most read, and possibly sometime I may try my hand at something of the kind." Eventually some of his adventures were told in marvelous, still popular books such as *My First Summer in the Sierra*, *Thousand Mile Walk to the Gulf*, *Stickeen*, and *The Story of My Boyhood and Youth*.

III

"Heaven bless her always."

Wanda celebrated her 13th birthday on March 25, 1894. She was amazingly mature and capable. She needed to be for the family depended on her, the strong, healthy one, to aid, cheer, counsel and listen. She was Mama's helper, Papa's companion, Grandma's shoulder, and sister's watchdog; a child of grace abounding in zest for life. She knew nothing but love and expressed it to others.

As much as Muir might have wanted Wanda along on some of his trips, he had to leave her at home as a balance wheel and a faithful reporter, in the household of fragile women.

During the years 1895-98, he kept a journal in which he made fatherly comments.

•

Jan. 23, 1895 . . . This is Helens birthday & she is greatly excited about it, for it marks she says, the end of her babyhood. She is 9 & says she will no longer answer to the name of Baby . . . She celebrated the day on the hills. She climbs well & is in perfect health. An unspeakable blessing after the extreme delicacy of her earliest years . . .

March 25 . . . Wanda's birthday—the 14th. Happy girl Heaven bless her always. I dread pain & trouble in so sweet & good a life.—If only death and pain could be abolished . . .

April 12 . . . Another lovely day mostly solid sunshine . . . Took a creeping thing . . .
glad to see love walking—flowers—trees & every bird & beast & creeping thing. . . .

•

In preparation for writing his guidebook to Yosemite, Muir made a trip to the Park to refresh his memories. Although *The Yosemite* wasn't published until 1912, the research took place in August of 1895.

•

Monday, Aug. 5

Dear Wanda.

I am just about to start afoot down the Tuolumne Canon. Yesterday I climbed Mt Conness with two young men who joined me at Yo Valley & have been good bright manly company. It is about noon & here at the foot of the Big Tuolumne Meadows we part, they returning to Yosemite & I to go alone through the canon to Hetch Hetchy & then to Crockers and thence to Yosemite & home. I suppose I will be about two weeks in the canon. I feel pretty well today after climbing & riding & crackers. My companions will lead back my horse & I will be free in the wilderness again in the old way, without blankets, but I think I can stand it about as well as ever. The flowers are lovely on the glacier meadows & on the high mountains & you will never know how glad I am to be with them again. I am sitting on a rock by the river & a cascade is chanting gloriously & all the old enthusiasm has come again.

I will have a hard grand trip & will be cold a little at night but will not suffer for I know well how to use a camp fire. I wrote to Helen before leaving Yosemite & will write your mother when I return. Love to all. How gloriously the river is singing, Ever affectionately your father

John Muir

•

Over the years, Muir had experienced premonitions, such as the forewarning of his father's last illness, that had proved true. Thus, in June 1896, when he sensed that his mother was ill, he boarded the next train for Portage. So sure was he that he wired his sister Mary to join him on the train in Kearney, Nebraska, where she lived, and the same to his brother Dan in Lincoln. Dan, a physician, was scornful of hunches, and refused, but Mary was persuaded.

When they arrived unannounced at their mother's home, she was sinking into a coma after a sudden attack, but rallied under the care and companionship of six of her eight children. Muir stayed until Dan arrived and agreed with the local doctor that Ann Muir was out of danger. Both assured Muir that it would be safe for him to travel on to Harvard University where he was to receive an honorary degree.

•

Portage, Wisconsin
June 11, 1896.

Dear Wanda & Helen.

This is a charming summer day. So many trees,—Oaks Elms Maples,—are planted in Portage it looks like a forest & the sunbeams are pouring through the green & yellow leaves & the birds are singing. It is all delightful. I saw two scarlet tanagers this morning red as coalfire, & more robins than I could count getting breakfast on a Mulberry tree before the door. They are tame because they are not disturbed by cats or dogs or guns. Four robins on the lawn were within 5 steps of my feet as I sat on the veranda. The tanagers are so red I think they would frighten California cats. It is just noon, & bells & whistles are making a jangling noise ridiculously big for so little a town. Joanna's babies are growing fast & I think you would like them. I gave them money to buy candy & told them to be sure to eat it all, & they marched down town right merrilly.

Helen, Marys girl, is just about your age Helen and is very bright. You would both like her also. She is a great fence & post climber, for there are no trees to climb in Kearney [Nebraska]. I hope you are not neglecting your lessons nor the garden & that you are careful in carrying candles.[1] I hope to write you another letter soon when I am not so dull as now. The cats no doubt are well. Have you got a dog yet?

Ever your father

John Muir

The Osborn Home on the Hudson
Sunday June 21, 1896

My dear Wanda.

Mr Johnson & I came up here last evening from New York & the change from deadly heat & dust to lovely woods & gardens & cool streams is delightful. Few homes could be more perfectly delicious in scenery & snowy linen & I'm glad of the rest to get ready for the Harvard day next Wednesday. Tomorrow I am going farther up the Hudson to meet Burroughs & spend a night & day with him. Then I go back to New York & thence go to Cambridge Tuesday after-

1. The Muirs used candles and kerosene lamps as they did not have electricity installed until 1914.

noon. But if Mother should be worse I would leave all & go to her.[1]

I got your letter dated June 11, yesterday forwarded from Portage & was very glad to get the news.

Very many flattering invitations are coming in but I can accept none in advance of news from Mother.

With love to you & all I am

Your affectionate father

Sylvan Lake Hotel
Custer, S.D., July 6, 1896

Hello Midge Hello Wanda!

My!! if you could only come here when I call you, how wonderful you would think this hollow in the rocky Black Hills is. It is wonderful even to me after seeing so many wild mountains, curious rocks rising alone or in clusters, gray & jagged & rounded in the midst of a forest of pines & spruces & poplars & birches, with a little lake in the middle & carpet of meadow gay with flowers. It is in the heart of the famous Black Hills where the Indians & Whites quarreled & fought so much. The whites wanted the gold in the rocks, & the Indians wanted the game—the deer & elk that used to abound here. As a grand deer pasture this was said to have been the best in America, & no wonder the Indians wanted to keep it for wherever the white man goes the game vanishes.

We came here this forenoon from Hot Springs 50 miles by rail & 12 by wagon. And most of the way was through woods fairly carpeted with beautiful flowers. A lovely red lily, Lilium Pennsylvanicum, was common, 2 kinds of spiraea & a beautiful wild rose in full bloom, anemones, calachortus, larkspur, etc. etc. etc. far beyond time to tell. . . . How sweet the air is! I would like to stop a long time & have you & Mama with me. What walks we would have!! We leave tonight for Edgemont.

Here are some mica flakes & a bit of spiraea I picked up in a walk with Prof. Sargent.

1. Ann Muir died in her sleep on June 23. The following day Muir received his degree at Harvard, then returned to Portage for her funeral. Afterwards, he made sentimental visits to friends in Madison, Milwaukee, and Indianapolis before joining the Forestry Commissioners in Chicago for an investigatory tour of U.S. forests. Charles S. Sargent, Professor William H. Brewer of Yale, Arnold Hague of the U.S. Geological Survey, and General Henry L. Abbot of the U.S. Engineer Corps were his companions.

Goodbye my babes. Sometime I must bring you here. I send love & hope you are well.

John Muir

Martinez, Calif.
July 10, 1896

Dear Papa:

We received your letter from Hot Springs yesterday and just a few minutes ago your other letter came with the flowers and mica in it and the picture at the top. It must be a most wonderful and beautiful place where you are and I hope some day that we may see it too. I hope that it is a good deal cooler where you are than it is here for it has been dreadfully hot for a long time. Everybody says that it is trying to make up for the cold weather last spring, but I think that it has done that already and that it is time to stop.

Three of the letters that we wrote you, two to Portage and one to New York, came back here. I will send them to you now so you will know what we were doing then too.

When are you coming home Papa? It seems such a very long time since you left us at the Martinez station and it is so strange for us to think how many different places you have been since then and of all that has happened in that short time. We received your letter which told about Grandma Muir's death, oh Papa, how I wish that I could have seen and known her.

We have been over to see Aunt Margaret very often. She is feeling much better than at first, but this weather is hard for her. We are all well. Helen does not mind the heat at all this summer.

Early this morning we walked over to Uncle David's and then we went up on the big east hill. We enjoyed the walk very much but the grass and flowers are all dry now. The corn and beans that we planted are growing finely.

Write to us as often as you can.

Lovingly,
Wanda

Martinez, California
July 20, 1896

My dear Papa:

Today is cool and delightful. A little foggy and with a fine west breeze blowing.

We received your letters from Helena and the Yellowstone and the dear little flowers that were with them. I wish that I could see some of the blue fringed gentians growing and the geysers and all the other things that are in the big kitchen where the water is always boiling. Mama says that would just suit her. She would like a place where the boiling water never fails!

You seem to miss the mosquitoes. Had you been here a few days ago you would have seen and felt all the "little blesseds" you cared to.

We are all well here. Helen is very well, lively and growing.

Aunt Margaret received your letter yesterday. She is about as well as usual again. She says your kind beautiful letters about Grandma Muir have comforted her greatly.

Miss Graydon came up to see Aunt Ette and of course came over here a while. She could not stay long but we enjoyed her visit very much. She is looking very well and will spend the rest of her vacation in Oakland.

The peaches are beginning to get ripe and we will have all we can eat in a day or two. The road up the valley is being sprinkled now and this morning Mr. Coleman had the road across the vineyard sprinkled.

We are very careful about fire and I think you need not worry about your notes. We do not cook a hot supper late in the evening so do not have any fire after four or five o'clock and very little even then.

Where shall we send our next letters? Mama and Helen will write to you tomorrow.

Lovingly,
Wanda Muir

•

During the last week of August and early September, Muir toured the West Coast with the Forestry Commission while they studied forests and timbering around Crater Lake, Crescent City, Ukiah and Eureka. Before they traveled to Southern California and the Grand Canyon, Muir was home for one night during which he "saw my wife and babies, changed clothing, repacked satchel ready to rejoin party next day."

•

Dear Papa.

Palace Hotel
Visalia, Cal. Sep. 17, 1896

My dear little Helen & Wanda & Mama.

The train started so soon that I had to hurry to jump on after talking half a minute to May & Jessie Reid. & so I did not get to the window to wave you a last goodbye for the trip. So you must excuse me, for I feel bad about it.

We had a pretty comfortable trip on the cars—not very hot or dusty. Mr. Magee & Tommie & Fred were on board on their way to Kings River Yosemite & I introduced them to our party & had good chat & talk.[1]

Tomorrow morning we get up at 4 & start at 5 for Mineral King on the Kaweah where the military camp is. It will be a very long ride of 59 miles of rough rocky dusty road, but much of the way will be through grand pines & firs & libocedrus, douglas spruce & Sequoia, & then everything has been pleasantly arranged for us. From here to the foothills we will ride in light surreys then we will change horses & ride the rest of the way in a stage with four horses & be accommodated with beds & everything by the officer in charge.

Now I must go to bed, Good night Happy dreams, Take good care of yourself dear Helen & God care for you & bless you all. Ever your loving friend & father,

John Muir

The Stollenbeck
Los Angeles, Cal.
Sep. 21, 1896

My darlings Helen & Wanda.

I slept last night in a box called a Pullman Upper & of course feel pretty stupid but I thought of you & Mama the first thing & so that shows I am quite well.

I wish you could have been with me up the mtns to see the pines & Silver Firs & brown giant Sequoias but the road was awful dusty & awful rough & bumpy, & awful long,—sixty miles Friday & 60

1. Thomas Magee, a San Francisco businessman, and avid mountaineer, had climbed Half Dome with Muir in July, 1877. His sons, Tom, Fred and Will, were also friends and trail companions on excursions with Muir. To Muir, a "Yosemite" was any deep, glacial-and-water cut canyon resembling Yosemite Valley, as did his destination, King's Canyon.

yesterday—besides all this railroad business is bunk. The soldiers took good care of us & we saw ten species of conifers & rocks & waterfalls many.[1]

Here are some silver fir seed wings and Eriogonum [buckwheat] etc.

With love my dears.

[John Muir]

•

Muir's service with the Forestry Commission was one of his most significant contributions to the conservation movement. The commission's report to President Cleveland urged creation of thirteen new reservations and two national parks (Rainier and Grand Canyon), scientific management of forests, and changes in timber and mining laws. Before his first term ended in March 1897, President Cleveland signed an order recommending the preservation of 21 million acres of land.

Caught off guard by the president's action, lumbermen, stockmen, miners and like-minded politicians spent the next year trying to kill the bill. Muir wrote vigorous, widely-read articles defending forests. "Through all the wonderful, eventful centuries since Christ's time—and long before that—God has cared for these trees . . . but he can not save them from fools—only Uncle Sam can do that."

Such words, such attacks on destructive practices, such impassioned eloquence won public sentiment, and the presidential order was finally upheld.

Muir made only one long trip in 1897 and that was to Alaska with Charles S. Sargent and botanist William Canby.

•

Martinez, Calif.
Aug. 7, 1897

Dear Papa:

I suppose you reached Bamph [Banff] yesterday and are enjoying yourself in a cooler climate than we have down here today, I hope. Helen has a light attack of the Whooping Cough but except when the coughing spells come on she feels well and is up all the time.

Grandma has been very sick since you left, but is feeling a little better this morning. The rest of the family are pretty well.

1. Army troops took custodial care of Sequoia, General Grant and Yosemite National Parks.

My eyes ached so much that I went to the City Saturday with Aunt Mary and had them tested and got some glasses. They are very uneven. My left eye is very nearsighted and the right one only a little bit so, since I got the glasses they have not hurt at all and do not get tired when I read or write or am out in the sun.

Aunt Mary is here and has begun painting.[1] She has done a good deal of sketching and has started to copy the Mt. Shasta picture [Wm. Keith]. Aunt Margaret is feeling better.

Have you finished your article yet? And where shall we send our next letters to you? Helen will write to you tomorrow. She says to tell you that the puppy is very well and has learned several new tricks but is getting more mischivous every day.

Everybody asks if you have gone to the Clondyke when they hear that you are not at home.

Will send you a letter from Mr. Johnson. The *Century* wants you to write a lot of articles for them instead of giving them to the *Atlantic*.

Write as often as you can and let us know what you are doing. I will write again in a day or two.

Affectionately your daughter

Wanda Muir.

•

Muir arrived home from Alaska in September to a gloomy household, for long-ailing Mrs. Strentzel, 76, was dying. Her death on September 24, 1897, left a void, for she had been greatly beloved.

C. S. Sargent and Canby invited Muir to inspect forests in the South with them the following autumn. He accepted enthusiastically. "I don't want to die without once more saluting the grand, godly, round-headed trees of the east side of America that I first learned to love and beneath which I used to weep for joy when nobody knew me." That experience had been chronicled in 1867, and was published in *A Thousand Mile Walk to the Gulf*. The 1898 trip was in some ways and places a nostalgic duplication. Once again a thorough immersion in nature rid him of a cough, and healed his spirit. Once more he was exuberant with love of life and wilds.

•

1. More than fifty years later Mary Muir Hand's distinctive portrait of her famous brother was given to the John Muir National Historic Site.

Courtesy of Sherry Hanna

Her grandmotherly appearance did not suggest the adventuresome life Louisiana E. Strentzel (1821-1897) had experienced in Tennessee, Texas, and California.

Cranberry Inn,
Cranberry, North Carolina
Sept. 22 1898

My dear Wanda.

. . . We arrived at this charming inn after dark in the rain tired out & more than half sick with bad food & overabundance of fine scenery, new flowers new trees etc. Just this moment Sargent who was out on the porch looking at the rain & magnolias, liquidambers, sassafras, rhododendron, liriodendron, chestnut oak & scarlet hemlock etc. came in & said "Muir, what are you writing? a romance?" I said "No. I am writing the truth" That said he is a very hard thing to do. "Yes" I said "I know it is for some"

. . . The rain continues & we may be here all day. I hope we will, for the views from the verandas are very fine. Mountains & waving hills rising in broad billows beyond each other all richly covered with the most beautiful trees. I would like to stay a year. How deliciously fresh the air is full of the scents of the woods.

I am to see Agassiz and Hunnewell so Sargent says & Page wants to show me the Boston writers.[1] He has a months nonsense cut out for me which of course must be cut down.

Page says the bird & beast articles are just right as they are & must be published immediately. He is to send the proof sheets of the birds to Biltmore . . .

Much love to all

Your loving father,

J.M.

Martinez, Calif.
Oct. 7, 1898

Dear Papa:

We have received your delightful lot of letters and telegrams and enjoyed them all so much. Your letter from Knoxville, Tenn. came yesterday. What a fine time you must be having! We were all very glad to hear that you were well again, for we had been worrying about you a good deal. We are all well here and are very careful about watching the fires. Aunt Margaret is about as usual, she received your letter with the lovely little heathwort blossoms in it,

---

1. Walter Hines Page was editor of the *Atlantic Monthly*, which published many articles by Muir.

and we always take our own over for she enjoys seeing them all so much.

It has rained several times lately and today there is a regular storm. It will be awful for the grapes for they are already cracking badly, but everything else is beautifully fresh and clear and clean and the grass is springing up everywhere . . .

Last Saturday eleven of us went over to the big Laurel. The views were grand. We could see the Sierra very clearly and the flowers and ferns are just starting up now. On another walk we found a little canyon back of Ferndale where there were thirty or forty quite large maple trees with red and yellow leaves. How beautiful whole forests must look in such gorgeous dress.

. . . There has been much blasting and banging away on the railroad cut.[1] We went up there Sunday and found a lot of fossil shells. There was one flat rock about three feet square that was just covered with different kinds of shells and Helen was very much pleased to find a petrified worm.

We have just received a letter from a lady who wants you to give a series of lectures before her club, and another from a young newspaper woman who wants you to tell her how the clam shells that were found in the tunnel managed to get there. She said that she was going to write them up and that as you were the greatest authority, she would like to get your views.

[Wanda]

•

Because Sargent became ill, the travelers retreated to Boston so he could recuperate at home. That gave Muir time to travel into Canada and back through New England which, he said, "was robed with glorious leaf colors." Muir's letters home, he explained in his lengthy October 28 missive, constituted little more than a record so he could "keep track of myself . . . "

•

1. A trestle, tunnel, and railbed were being built by the Santa Fe Railroad about a quarter of a mile south of the Muir home. When completed the nearby station was named Muir Station.

Van Ness House
On Lake Champlain
Burlington, Vt., Oct. 18 1898

Dear Wanda and Helen, and Mamma.

I'm pretty sleepy, for it was after midnight when I went to bed last night & the bed was only a confounded stuffy jiggling bunk at the top of a sleeping or sleepless car. But this day was so crisp & bright & delightful, so full of lovely & wild scenery it might awaken the dead & do away with sleep altogether. I stopped here on my way from Montreal to the White Mountains & all the scenery was beautiful & must be beautiful all the year but robed with glorious leaf colors as it is now nobody can half tell or even hint it . . . I got here about noon, had a nice dinner in a fine clean commodious hotel which you may be sure I appreciated after the squalid piggy places we had to stop at in the southern states. Then I got a buggy & drove through the pretty town & the hills, & along the lake through the midst of yellow & purple & golden trees & bushes. My! if you & Helen & Mamma could have been with me. Tomorrow I start for Stowe & thence up Mt Mansfield. Thence I go to Mt Washington & the passes & notches of the White Mountains, & then back to Boston, perhaps passing through a part of the State of Maine.

You & Helen must read or reread Parkmans history of the Indians & early French explorers in Canada. You will find charming descriptions of this region in the midst of the grim & red history of the savages missionaries & adventurous traders. Lakes George & Champlain were the highway to Canada for both Indians & Whites for centuries.

You may be sure Ill sleep long & well tonight. I have a good room & a good bed. I wonder if John Swett is still here-abouts. How he must have enjoyed his New Hampshire hills.[1] Give my love to Maggie. Heaven bless you all, so prays

J.M.

1. Swett, Muir's close friend and neighbor in Alhambra Valley, had been born and raised in New Hampshire. Later he became California Superintendent of Schools. Before his marriage, Muir had spent winter months in the Swett's San Francisco home. Mary and John prodded Muir into writing down his experiences and opinions.

Martinez, Calif.
Oct. 23, 1898

Dear Papa:

I suppose that by this time you are in New York or Boston or somewhere near them and that you are having a fine time, but I hop that you will not like them well enough to stay quite as long as you say Prof. Sargent wants you to.

We have not received any letters from you for several days but we have enjoyed the ones from Knoxville, Chattanooga, Huntsville and all the other places so much, and your descriptions of the wonderful forests that you have seen. I wish so much that I could be with you and see them all too, but it will be fine to have you tell us all about your trip when you get home.

Everybody here is as well as usual. Helen is very well and happy but wishes very much that she could see you: she has just come in from teaching Stickeen tricks and is studying her Bible lesson now.

We have been having delightful weather, but this morning it looks as if it might rain before night. Everyone has been hurrying off grapes lately, but they were very badly hurt by the first rains.

A great deal of grading has been done on the railroad and the little tunnel back of the house is in a long way, a good deal of track is down near here and we can hear the cars buzzing back and forth all the time.

How did it seem to you to be traveling where you took your long walk 32 years ago, did the country look the same as it did then?

How soon do you think that you will be home?

Hoping you are well.

Your loving daughter,
Wanda Muir

Albemarle Hotel
New York
Oct 28, 98

My dear Wanda.

I've been trying to tell you the course of my wanderings since I left home partly that I might thus help to keep track of myself. I've been going so fast & have made so many turns & doubles far & near in so many states north & south—enjoyed so much & been bothered & fussed so much—mixed day & night so much in cars, hotels, friends homes steamboats shanties etc it is no easy matter to keep anything like a clear record.

I think I wrote last from Burlington, Vermont. From there I went to Stowe Vt... Thence in wind & rain & fog drove in buggy 17 miles through Smugglers Notch to railroad, thence through beautiful hills woods & mountains & villages all luminous with autumn purple & gold to the White Mountains, so celebrated down through the famous Crawfords Notch & on down derry down to Portland Maine... Thence on & on through the Maine & Canada woods to Quebec. Thence south again through I dont know how many states & across I dont know how many rivers & lovely colored landscapes to Boston arriving there last Sunday morning in time for breakfast at Sargent's....

Next day went to Page in Boston. Talked an hour with Mifflin... was guided through the huge bookmaking establishment at Riverside etc.[1] Next day went to the Arnold Arboretum & library thence to Boston again, thence to Cambridge & spent the night at Page's home & visited Mrs Gray & talked over old botanic times etc.[2]... Yesterday too when Sargent, a friend of his & I were at lunch the waiter brought me your last letter & the clippings on a silver plate, & when I got back from Quebec I found all yours & Helens & Mammas letters at Sargents, he having had them forwarded from N.Y. so now I feel better. Yesterday forenoon I saw all the Century people. ... the Columbia College Museum where all the tree sections are & Mrs Sargents drawings of the flowers & cones etc. Also the paleontological collections & heaven knows what else. Here I found Prof. Osborn & he is to take me to the Hudson River home next Monday or Thursday. Then we drove through Central Park. Thence I went to the Century office & Johnson took me home to dinner calling on Tesla at his laboratory on the way.[3] He (Tesla) wants us to

---

1. Editor Page influenced Muir to let the Houghton Mifflin Company, owners of the Riverside Press, become his publisher, succeeding the Century Company. Later Page was a partner in the publishing firm of Doubleday, Page and Company. Despite his desertion of the Century firm, Muir and Johnson remained the closest of friends.

2. Asa Gray's widow. Gray, Harvard's famed botanist, had spent a week botanizing in Yosemite in 1872. Afterwards, Muir and Gray maintained a friendship by correspondence. Gray named a species of a wild flower, *Ivesia muirii*, for Muir, its collector.

3. Nikola Tesla was the inventor of the Tesla coil, the Tesla oscillator and other items basic to electricity. Robert Underwood Johnson considered him a genius, and knew he and Muir, with his inventive background, would be kindred spirits.

dine with him & spend an evening at the Waldorf, a swallowtail affair I fear. This afternoon I am to go with Gilder to his summer home in the Berkshire Hills for a few days. Then to Osborns. Sargent . . . wants me to return to Brookline & in eight or ten days go with him to Key West Florida. I would like to see Florida again. If I go it will be 3 or 4 weeks before I get home. I'll be precious glad to get to quiet work in the home nest once more. I seem to have been away a whole blurry indefinite year or half dozen of them. Were I to accept all the invitations that offer I would never get home at all or do another stroke of work.

The Sierra animals will be published soon, & Im now correcting the proofs of the birds.

Johnson is well & as funny as ever. He marched me through the wildest madest parts of the town last night, pretending he was taking me to jail for vagrancy—stopping now & then to ask little ragged boys the way to the police station—took me out into the middle of the streets among the whirl of cars & pretended he was afraid he would be run over to frighten me—showed me the moon & minutely told me how to know it among the million electric lights etc. & the way he fooled with Tesla was too funny for anything.

Lovingly yours Helen Mamma Maggie all

John Muir

•

It was while being pampered at the Osborn's "charming home . . . in the hushed tranquill woods" bordering the Hudson River that Muir realized how far he had traveled physically, socially and professionally. He wrote Helen about dainty linen on a soft bed where coffee was brought him by a servant. Outside a red squirrel seemed to scold, "Oh John Muir, camping, tramping tree-climbing scrambler! Churr, Churr! Why have you left us? Chirp Churr. who would have thought it?"[1]

A few days later, he wrote his wife, "Dear Lassie, it is settled that I go on a short visit to Florida with Sargent . . . " She urged him to stop first in Washington, D.C., "It would be grand if you could preach of God's forests to President McKinley. It does seem to be your duty to go . . . " Correspondence reveals that he did visit the capitol, but does not mention any appointment at the White House.[2]

1. November 4, 1898 letter.
2. *Son of the Wilderness, The Life of John Muir* by Linnie Marsh Wolfe, 1945, pages 278-79.

[Ca. Nov. 1898]

My dear Papa:

I have just received your letter from New York and we have all enjoyed the account of your lively wanderings very much. What a wonderful lot of beautiful places you must have seen. I do wish that I were with you and seeing them all too, but I should think that you would get dreadfully tired rushing around from one end of the country to the other. We will not be much surprised to get a letter from you from almost anywhere now.

The *Atlantic* came last night and we have been reading your animal article in it today.[1] It is fine . . .

I am glad to hear that our letters reached you at last, but it seems rather funny to think of serving them on silver plates as part of your dinner.

It seems a long time since we saw you. Don't stay away too dreadfully long.

Your loving daughter,
Wanda Muir

•

In November Muir traveled to Florida with Charles Sargent, and wrote enthusiastic letters home describing the trees, the fall color and his nostalgic reunion with the woman who had nursed him through malaria in 1867.

•

Key West, Florida.
Nov. 17, 1898.

My dear Helen and Wanda

Its very hot here & I feel a little dull & sleepy mostly from scant allowance of sleep. The night before last there was a fashionable ball at the hotel & the music was horrid loud & kept me awake till 3 in the morning when they played Sweet Home & went to it. Then yesterday we hired a sloop & sailed over the blue water to the Marquesas Keys for palms, 2 new species & my! werent the palms exuberant & the sand flies & mosquitoes & fiddler-crabs also. We got back against a head wind about 11 oclock pretty tired. We saw lots of birds & fishes & flowers. The palms & mangroves are all twined & tangled with flowery vines & it was a hot job & a prickly

1. Muir's article "Among the Animals of the Yosemite" appeared in the November, 1898 *Atlantic* magazine.

job getting through them. The color of the water was charming—green & blue & purple & bronze brown & gold. We go back to Miami tonight on steamer thence across to the West Coast by rail, thence back to Jacksonville, thence home by New Orleans.

Im glad I'm turning homeward at last though Ill miss Sargent Love to Mamma & Maggie & the very darlings Soon Ill see you. Goodby once more Sargent is in a hurry

[John Muir]

•

Homecoming in late November was happy, but the succeeding months, he confided to Page, disappointing. "I lost half the winter in a confounded fight with sheep & cattlemen & politicians on behalf of forests. During the other half I was benumbed & interrupted by sickness in the family, while in word works, even at the best, as you know, I'm slow as a glacier."

In April, however, when he received an invitation to join railroad tycoon Edward H. Harriman's scientific expedition to Alaska, he almost refused. After all, he had been to Alaska, and he was suspicious of being indebted to any businessman.[1] Dr. C. Hart Merriman, director of the Biological Survey, persuaded him that Harriman's intents were noble, and the company of the highest caliber. Indeed the prestigious guests included "twenty-three of the country's top scientists representing twelve fields, three artists, two photographers, two physicians, two taxidermists, and one chaplain."[2] Poet Charles Keeler, naturalists Muir and John Burroughs, the Harriman family, and an attentive ship's crew enlarged the party to 126. Keeler was Muir's cabinmate, and Burroughs, who Muir said "growled at and snarled at the good Bering Sea and me," his favorite target for banter. Burroughs retaliated in verse and the statement, "In John Muir we had an authority on glaciers, and a thorough one—so thorough he would not let the rest of the party have an opinion on the subject."

Keeler wrote his wife that Muir was such a great talker that he had "little time to myself."[3] Muir loved to discourse on glaciers, to argue, and to explore. He did all three on board and ashore during the two-month expedition, plus contributing to the general enjoyment of the passengers and making many new friends. In retrospect, he wrote

---

1. *Looking Far North* by William H. Goetzmann and Kay Sloan, published by The Viking Press, New York, 1982, p. 10.
2. Ibid., p. 14.
3. Ibid., p. 27.

Harriman's daughters: "To me it [the trip] was peculiarly grateful & interesting because nearly all my life I have wandered & studied alone. On the *Elder* I found not only the fields I liked best to study, but a hotel, a club, & a home, together with a floating university in which I enjoyed the instruction & companionship of a lot of the best fellows imaginable . . . "

His many letters home revealed his pleasure in nature and man. Two are quoted. Unfortunately, Wanda's replies are missing.

•

Sitka June 14, 1899

Dear Louie and bairns.

We are just entering Sitka Harbor after a delightful sail down Peril Straits & a perfectly glorious time in Glacier Bay—5 days of the most splendid weather I ever saw in Alaska. I was out 3 days with Gilbert & Palache revisiting the glaciers at the upper end of the bay.[1] Great changes have taken place. The Pacific Glacier has melted back 4 miles & changed into 3 separate glacier each discharging bergs in grand style. One of them unnamed & unexplored, I named last evening in a lecture they made me give in the Social Hall The Harriman Glacier which was received with hearty cheers. After the lecture Mr Harriman came to me & thanked me for the great honor I had done him. It is a very beautiful gl. the front discharging bergs like the Muir about 3/4 of a mile wide on the sea wall.

Everybody was delighted with Glacier Bay & the grand Muir Glacier, watching the beautiful bergs born in thunder—parties scattered out in every direction in row boats & steam & naphtha launches on every sort of quest. John Burroughs & Charlie Keeler climbed the mountain on the East side of Muir Gl. 3000 feet & obtained grand view far back over the mountain to the glorious Fairweather Range. I tryed hard to get out of lecturing but was compelled to do it. All seemed pleased. Lectures every night. The company all goodnatured & harmonious. Our next stop will be Yakutat.

I'm all sunburned by three bright days among the bergs. I often wish you could have been with us. You will see it all some day. Heaven bless you. Remember me to Maggie.

Goodbye

[John Muir]

1. Explorer-scientist Grove Karl Gilbert and mineralogist Charles Palache.

Kodiak, [Alaska] July 3 [18]99

Darlings Wanda & Helen. I have often thought how fine it would be to have you on this trip. The Harriman & Averil girls & Miss Draper about your own ages enjoy it so much & have so bright & merry & instructive time.[1] So many grand mountains with birds & flowers & glaciers & waterfalls & so many wise men to tell them about all they see. Everyday is delightful & even when we were out on the open ocean the ship was so steady nobody was seriously sea-sick a single hour. Some day you will see the Alaska islands & glaciers & mountains & forests . . . Yesterday I climbed a green flower mountain back of the town 1500 ft high & it is one flower bed all the way to the top. I wish I could send you a big handful I brought down all fresh . . . I did not get so tired as I would climbing Mt Wanda for I am getting stronger now & eat three or four times as much as at home. It seems very queer to have so many companions on a glacial excursion after being alone so much. Still, I'm lonely to see you. I often wonder what you are doing & how Stickeen & Tom are getting along. It is light all the time & I dont think Ive seen a star since we were at Sitka. It is often eleven or twelve o'clock before I go to bed. & we are going farther north yet before we start for home. John Burroughs is delighted with the birds here most of them are singing now. They came many of them from California & Mexico. Even the little ruby throated humming bird is here tho the little fairy muggins had to fly all the way from Mexico or Central America since spring. One of the Zonotrichea, so common about our house in winter the one with yellow on his brow is here & have built their nests & some have young already. The naturalists call it the golden crowned Sparrow . . . It is a sad sight to see the naturalists a dozen of them at once shooting every kind of bird whether they have young or not, even the humming birds, and the mammal hunters set out 100 or 200 traps at once to catch mice marmots shrews etc. & then comes skinning & stuffing a horrid business.[2] They all make fun of me about glaciers but I dont mind the fun of course. Ill soon be home. Good night darlings. Give Tom something whenever he asks it.

---

1. Mary, Cornelia and Carol were Harriman's daughters, Elizabeth Averell his niece and Dorthea Draper a friend. Muir delighted in the girls' company and corresponded with them after the trip. He dubbed them the "Big Four" and Harriman's sons, Roland and Averell, who were also aboard, the "Little Two."

2. Specimen collecting was an important, if dismaying, goal for some of the scientists.

John Muir National Historic Site Collection

Now the focus of the nearly nine acre John Muir National Historic Site, the "Big House" was the showpiece of the 2,600-acre Strentzel-Muir ranch.

IV

". . . unstoppable as an avalanche . . ."

During 1900 and 1901, there was a curious dearth of letters from Wanda to "Dear Papa" or from Papa to her. Muir, who was the kindest of fathers, and strongly believed in education, did not believe in college for women, at least his girls. He, the most independent of men, seemed to believe that a woman's place was in her parents' home until marriage, and, after that, in her husband's home! Subconsciously he may have felt, as indeed had been the case, that Wanda was Helen's guardian; that her desire to go away to school was a betrayal. Evidence for this editorial belief is partly the very lack of documentation, the sudden cessation of loving letters between father and daughter. This opinion was advanced by Jean Hanna Clark, who had had discussions with her mother regarding Muir's Victorian attitudes.

In an October, 1901, letter to Katherine Graydon, who had tutored his daughters, Muir made a rather unflattering assessment of his eldest. Wanda, he said, "is going to school, and expects soon to enter the University. She is a faithful, steady scholar, not in the least odd or brilliant, but earnest and unstoppable as an avalanche."

Greta Variel, a sorority sister, was far more complimentary, writing that Wanda "was all but bursting with love," and marveling that after her unconventional schooling, she could prepare herself for college in only eighteen months at a formal institution.[1] To be accepted by the University of California at Berkeley, Wanda needed some traditional schooling to make up for what she had missed during the years of informal, home-directed studies. John Muir may not have agreed, but Louie did, and the prestigious Anna Head School, close to the university campus, was chosen.

Late in December of 1899, three months short of her nineteenth birthday, Wanda, who had never attended any organized school, rarely been away from Alhambra Valley, and never opposed her father, left home alone on the Santa Fe train that crossed the Muir vineyards, for Berkeley.

A series of letters to "Dear Mama" at once illustrate a rift with her father, and her calm, joyful adjustment to school and culture. As usual, "Dear Mama's" replies are missing, but their caring content can be guessed at from some of Wanda's comments.

•

Jan. 2, 1900

Dear Mama:

I reached here safely and have a very comfortable room with Hazel Picher. There are ten other new girls. I have lived through a Latin and History recitation and did *not* get scared.

I am a senior so can enter College as a regular in a year. Miss Head would not let me leave out Algebra, but there are two other girls about my age who are also beginning it, so there are only us three in the class and I will have plenty of time to make it all up in the year, so it will not make me stay here any longer.[2]

I like the girls and teachers very much.

Only had five minutes for this. Bell is ringing.

With love, Wanda

Berkeley, Sunday Evening [ca. 1900]

Dear Mama:

I have spent a quiet Sunday here today, went to church in the morning and rested most of the afternoon, but it did seem all day

1. "Wanda Muir Hanna," mss. by Greta Augustine Variel, loaned by Sherry (Mrs. Strentzel) Hanna.

2. Anna Head (1857-1932), daughter of a San Mateo County judge, was the ninth woman to graduate from the University of California. Her school, founded in 1887, was the most prominent female academy in Berkeley for eighty years. Since 1971, it has operated in Oakland as the coeducational Head-Royce School. Philosopher Josiah Royce was Miss Head's brother-in-law.

as if I ought to see you all. During the week I have so little time that I don't think much about it, but on Saturday and Sunday my thoughts are always with you—even if I am not.

O, how I wish that you could have been with me last night at the opera. It was perfectly wonderful and I did enjoy it so much. I like Nordica much better than I did Melba. She doesn't have conscious airs or many fancy trills, but seems to be singing perfectly and naturally, yet you can hear her glorious voice to the farthest corners of the house. de Reszke and the others are wonderfully fine too. You must try to hear them. I have a ticket for next Saturday night also. I would give you that, but it is way up in the second gallery. I can either go home next Friday evening and come back Saturday, or go home Sunday morning and come back Monday, which ever you would rather have me do, but I will surely be home for a little while, and then the next week I will be at home for four and a half days!

The weather last night was horribly sloppy, both the air and the streets were just as wet as they could possibly be. Some of the girls who insisted on wearing long skirts were pretty well soaked by the time they reached home, but as I wore my thick short skirt and heavy shoes and jacket I didn't mind it at all.

Is Aunt Margaret feeling any better than when Helen wrote? And how are you? Don't work so hard. It must have been awful for Papa to have so many teeth taken out at once. I hope he is able to eat something besides "spoon vittles" by this time.

The box of flowers and good things to eat was much enjoyed. I still have a good many nice lemons left, and the geraniums are still fresh, but all the other things are gone ...

My lessons have been easy this week, so I have been able to learn them without any trouble notwithstanding all the other things that have been going on. I am *very well* and have *not* got a cold and am *not* getting up early in the morning so you need not worry any about me. The lights are going out—so I will have to stop this scribbling. It seems as if I always have to finish my letters in a dreadful hurry. I thought I had plenty of time tonight, but I was interrupted several times and in about a minute the room will be in total darkness, so—

Good night. Let me know when you think I had better come home.

Lovingly, Wanda

P.S. Next morning

Could you send me some red berries and any other red and green leaves that would be sure to get here Wednesday noon. If you send them so they would start Tuesday night they would get here in time. We want them to decorate for the tea on Wednesday. Do not send them unless they can start on the halfpast four train on Tuesday. We expected some other decorations, but have just found that we can not get them.

•

By January, 1901, Wanda entered the University of California as a freshman, and soon was pledged to Gamma Phi Beta sorority. Her bubbling letters to "Dear Mama" continued, indicating that Papa was still disapproving. Greta Variel recorded, "At that time John Muir thought college life unsuitable for girls, though of her defiance of his stern Scotch dictum, and of her persistence, he was later very proud." Wanda's letters exhibited her passion for music, interest in cultural activities, and enjoyment of sorority life. Her warmth and zest made her so popular that later she was elected president of the house.

•

Berkeley, Sunday morning

Dear Mama

I am now a real Gamma Phi Beta.[1] I was initiated last night and am still alive and in my usual good health. I thought some of going home this morning, but as I was up so late last night and all the nights this week I thought I had better rest today especially as I expect this week to be a very busy one too . . .

What I did last night will mean a great deal to me all through my college life, more than you know, so in spite of the fact that I am very sleepy and that I have just had two ex's [exams] and am expecting three more, I am very happy.

Did I get any kind of Sierra Club invitation for this Saturday and Sunday? I got a letter from the irrepressible Miss Hittell asking me if I had accepted [an invitation].[2]

1. Gamma Phi Beta was established at the University of California in April 1894. Eta Chapter house, where Wanda lived, was at 2429 Channing Street.

2. Katherine Hittel, niece of historian Theodore Hittel, was an active and charter member of the Sierra Club.

Holt-Atherton Pacific Center for Western Studies

After only nine months of formal education, Wanda, "a faithful, steady scholar," graduated from the prestigious Anna Head School in Berkeley and entered the University of California.

Yosemite Research Library Collection

Muir had loved Tuolumne Meadows from his first visit in 1869. Wanda shared his passion after her "comfortable and blissful" baptism there in 1901.

Sunday Evening, Feb. 17 [1901]
Berkeley, Cal.

Dear Mama:

This is Sunday afternoon and except for a little [violin] practicing, I haven't done anything all day but rest, which has been a decided change from what I have been doing all the rest of the week. This last week has been the liveliest and busiest one since I have been down here, but I've been having a perfectly beautiful time and intend to study this next week mostly, so don't think I'm getting too giddy . . .

Friday evening I went over to Dr. Ritter's for dinner and had a very nice time.[1] Mr. and Mrs. Keeler were there and a Mr. Barret who goes to college and I think boards there.[2] Prof. Ritter has just returned from a trip to Washington and other parts of the east so he talked about his trip, and the Keelers told about their long one. Later Friday evening Edna and I went to Oakland and heard Hoffman and enjoyed the music so much that we didn't mind at all the fact that the rain just poured both while we were going and coming. Hoffman plays some kinds of music nearly as well as Paderewski (how do you spell it?) but when he plays very loud he pounds too much, but altogether it was glorious. I enclose a program and have marked the ones I liked best . . .

Tuesday evening was the party and Tuesday afternoon the [sorority] tea which I told you about before. The house looked very pretty decorated with violets and smila and there were a great many people here although it rained most of the time. I don't know what we would have done if it had been clear for the four hundred people who came simply packed the house. I poured chocolate and handed round cakes to most of them so I was very much aware of the largeness of the number. I wish you could have been here and seen it all. The next time we have anything of the kind you just must come. I met Dr. Jepson at the tea and don't like him any better than I did

1. Dr. Mary Bennett Ritter was the university's first woman physician. Her husband, William E. Ritter, a member of the Harriman Expedition to Alaska, was chairman of the zoology department.

2. After the Harriman Expedition, Charles Keeler and his wife, Louise, were friends of the Muirs, and entertained Wanda in their Berkeley home.

before, although he has been quite amiable to me ever since.[1] The Hittells did not come, but everyone else I knew did.

I enclose a scrap of the ribbon I wore Tuesday with my white dress. It exactly matched the color of the carnations and looks much better by gaslight than in the day time.

Besides all these things that I did go to there was this week also the art exhibit in the city, the reception to Mrs. Hearst, a rally and the Carnot (?) debate, all of which I wanted to go to, but simply could not find the time for I had to do *some* studying, to say nothing of that ex in Political Economy . . .[2]

Lovingly, Wanda

Dear Mama:

I will be home Saturday evening at the usual time and will then tell you all the things that I have been doing throughout this rather busy week, and also add my mighty strength to the dog and gun protective arrangement that Helen wrote about.

I have just come from a class in Political Econ in which there are about 350 people. What do you think of that? I think I will like it very much. All my classes are nice except that Botany with Dr. Jepson. Still, that may not be so bad for Mr. Gardner has it half the time and he seems to be quite human, and there are a lot of nice people I know in the class.

I had an interview with Mrs. Magee about my cinch notice, and apart from making up *seven* cuts she is not going to make me do anything dreadful. I didn't think a two was particularly good in Greek History at first, but I found out yesterday that just exactly half of the class failed in that ex, so I'm beginning to feel quite proud of it, also pretty well pleased with my three in English History as only four people in the class got two's and there were no ones. Dr. Ritter's Medical course is lots of fun . . .

•

The months of Wanda's emacipation coincided with a period of good health for Helen and persistent writing for their father. He

1. Botanist Willis L. Jepson, whose books are still bibles to botanists, was also a charter member of the Sierra Club.
2. Phoebe Apperson (Mrs. George) Hearst was a generous guardian angel of the university.

spent a great deal of time in his "scribble den," and one result, *Our National Parks*, was well-received after its publication in 1901.

Once Wanda was at home for the summer, she and her father shared their old congeniality. His disapproval of her educational ambitions was muted if not lessened. Both girls were thrilled when, as so long promised, he invited them to accompany him and William Keith on a camping trip to Yosemite. It was no ordinary jaunt, but the first of the Sierra Club's large, well-organized Outings. The base camp for the 96 participants was Tuolumne Meadows, scene of many of Muir's solo ramblings in the 1870s. Despite the vast contrasts to his primitive camps, his enjoyment of the new venture was obvious as indicated in Wanda's letters to her mother.

By mid-July, 1901, Muir, 63; Keith, 62; Wanda, 20; and Helen, 15, had reached Crocker's Station, a popular mountain inn on the Big Oak Flat Road near the Yosemite boundary.

•

Crocker's, July 14

Dear Mama:

We reached here yesterday after a most delightful trip. Helen and I were the only people on the whole stage who were not the least bit tired and who enjoyed it tremendously and we have been perfectly happy ever since. Up here one not only feels well, but it seems as if every separate part of you feels separately and individually comfortable and blissful.

This is a beautiful place and these great trees are glorious and the air fine. Papa looks like another person since he got up here and rested all yesterday afternoon. He didn't cough at all this morning and is just bubbling over with fun. We are the jolliest crowd you ever saw . . .

We will be able to get and send letters once in a while as all Dr. Merriam's mail will be sent here, but you may not hear from us again for a week or more.[1] We are going to start tomorrow and go as far as the bad condition of the road will let us.[2] We heard just now that we could probably get through to the meadows in about five days, but anyway it doesn't matter much where we are for it is all fine . . .

1. After the Harriman Expedition, Merriam and Muir remained good friends as well as mountaineering companions.

2. Built in 1883 to service mines near Tioga Pass, the Tioga Road was abandoned, as were the mines, a year or so later. Until 1915, when it was rehabilitated, fallen trees, rocks and bridge-less creeks made it difficult to traverse.

[Camp Muir]
Tuolumne Meadows, July 16

A long, lank Kentuckian named Burkes, Papa and I stayed at the first camp that night and started down the [Tuolumne] canyon very early the next morning, tramped, slid, or crawled as the case might be, all day over awful rocks and through fearful brush, saw the most wonderfully glorious views, had a grand storm in the afternoon, got back to our night camp where the horses were at seven, and back here to the Meadows about nine that same night. Three tired, but very happy mortals. All the people in camp at once tried to find things for us to eat, and built a big fire for us to get dry by. After I had supper I felt as well as ever, and after having slept the sleep of the just that night, would have been glad to do it again the next day.

Papa and Mr. Burkes were alright too, although they stayed in camp and slept most of that day, but the three others who went in did not know the way so well and were awfully tired and scratched up by the rocks and brush.

Helen had gone on all the other trips and enjoys every minute she is here. We are going up on Unicorn Mountain tomorrow and she will tell you about that.

There are a great many pretty little squirrels and chipmunks all around camp, which are so gentle and full of curiousity that they will almost let you touch them. If you whistle to them they will listen with the greatest interest and enjoyment for half an hour or more at a time.

•

From the meadows, on July 20, Muir wrote glowingly to Louie, ". . . ye gods, what a jolting we got getting here in our six mule and horse chariot from Crockers to this mountain paradise!!! Only the girls endured it unscathed, laughed at it, giggled at it, and enjoyed it. Wanda and Helen take to this life in the rocks and woods like ducks to water as if born to it. No one could guess that this was their first mountaineering." In another letter, he bragged, "The girls are capital travelers and took naturally to mountaineering, climbing, scrambling, jumping—thinking nothing of walking 25 or 30 rock miles a day."

In turn, Wanda and Helen were thrilled with their father's forest demeanor, his sense of fun, unquenchable enthusiasm, and leadership qualities. Of course they knew he was an important man, but at Tuolumne Meadows they observed the deference and respect shown him by the assemblage. He was the magnet of the Outing. In retrospect one member wrote that John Muir was "guide and apostle . . . [whose] gentle, kindly face, genial blue eyes, and quaint, quiet observations on present and past conditions impressed us unforgettably."[1]

Papa, who his daughters regarded possessively but matter-of-factly, belonged not just to them but to the world.

Before returning to Martinez, Muir took them to Yosemite Valley, and introduced them to the splendor of his old haunts. After that mountain baptism, Wanda and Helen became addicts. In 1902, the Muirs joined the multitudinous crowd of nearly 200 Sierra Club members on an Outing in Kings Canyon.

Muir recalled the five weeks there as a "memorable ramble, merry and nobly elevating, and solemn in the solemn aboriginal woods and gardens of the great mountains—commonplace, sublime, and divine . . . a good trip in which everybody was a happy scholar at the feet of Nature, and all learned something direct from earth and sky, bird and beast, trees, flowers, and chanting winds and waters . . . "[2]

Wanda's description, written during the Outing, was less literary, but nonetheless refreshing.

•

Camp Colby,[3] July 5, 1902

Dear Mama:

We are spending the day in camp for the first time since we reached here. That is, this is the first whole day we have stayed in camp for there has been so much to see and so many places to go. I have just finished lunch. It consisted of ten biscuits, seven pickles (small) a big plate full of stewed dried apples, some flour and bacon grease gravy and a big dipper full of strong tea without sugar (sugar has given out) and am still living and feeling as happy and healthy as a mountaineer should. And so is Helen although she also ate a lot of ham besides all the things I did. This morning was spent in washing clothes and visiting around camp, and now I am lying on a bank of pine needles under a big yellow pine writing this letter. How I wish that you could be here for it is a fine place to rest and be lazy in as

1. "Camp Muir at Tuolumne Meadows," by Ella M. Sexton, *Sierra Club Bulletin*, Jan., 1902.

2. Oct. 12, 1902, Muir's letter to Anna R. Dickey.

3. Camp Colby in Kings Canyon was named for William E. Colby, an indefatigable mountaineer who served the Sierra Club as its secretary and Outing leader for many years.

well as to walk in. It is rather dry and dusty as you have no doubt guessed by the looks of this paper, but the weather has been delightful all the time and the grand domes and cliffs, the big trees and the beautiful river more beautiful even than either the Merced or Tuolumne, make it an ideal place to camp. One does not realize how many people are here unless one helps wash dishes or doles out soup to the hungry multitude. There are now nearly two hundred people in the canyon, rather too many to be in one camp, but still everything is simply marvelous. There never seems to be any rush or hurry, yet all the work of this big camp is done with the regularity and precision of clock work. The three Chinamen who do the cooking never seem particularly busy, yet we ate 57 big loaves of bread yesterday, for one meal we had hard tack . . .

Yesterday evening everyone tried to make as much noise as possible in celebrating the glorious fourth and a terrific racket was the result. Then we had a big bonfire rally, fire crackers, music and a wonderful supper of plum pudding, chocolate cake, nuts, olives, clam chowder, etc. etc. The whole affair must have been a tremendous surprise to the three gray squirrels and the other little animals that play around the camp, and even the echoes that the big rocks sent back had a startled and unnatural sound.

The only really hard side trip we have taken was the one to Goat Mt. which was tremendous in every sense of the word. Twenty-eight out of the 50 people who started from camp reached the top, 11 of whom were girls, Helen and I among the number, but it was Helen who covered herself with glory by reaching the top first and she did it without any effort. With those long slow *looking* strides of hers and was not at all tired after it. She has been the pet of the camp ever since and the number of trout, pieces of chocolate, cheese, jam and lemonade which is bestowed upon her daily is really alarming, but she is getting fat so I guess it's good for her . . .

Do please *write* if only a word or two and let me know how you are and what's going on at home. Has my Poly Con report come yet? or any other college reports or news? Speaking about college, what do you think? Yesterday we had a meeting of college women here in camp. It was held on the top of a big granite boulder and there were 60 college women, including both alumni and undergraduates, and representing about twenty different colleges. Twenty-seven of us were frat girls. Isn't that a pretty good showing for a place like this, and isn't it a fine answer to the people who say that college girls are weak and good for nothing generally? for there wasn't one of us that could not comfortably walk twenty miles, or if necessary do anything that has to be done around a camp from cooking a camp meal to packing a mule.

Miss Jordan, President Jordan's daughter, is one of the most delightful people I have met up here.[1] (There are a lot of Berkeley people here and I have met several of my own class at college whom I had never happened to meet there.) Helen Swett is a fine camper and she and her guitar are very much appreciated around the campfire in the evening.[2]

Good night,

Lovingly, Wanda

1. David Starr Jordan was the first president of Stanford University. Jordan had three daughters; the one mentioned was probably Edith, the eldest.
2. Helen Swett, whose name was suggested by Muir, was born in 1874 while Muir was living with the John Swett family in San Francisco.

V

"... lovingly, your very happy daughter ..."

As soon as her classes at Berkeley were over in early May of 1903, Wanda went home and soon began packing for another Club Outing in Yosemite—this time, to Hetch Hetchy Valley. Helen was going, but not their father, for he planned to take a round-the-world trip with his botanist friend, Charles Sargent. Their ship passage from New York was set before a personal letter from President Theodore Roosevelt urging Muir to accompany him on a trip to Yosemite changed his mind. Muir wrote Sargent, "I might be able to do some forest good in talking freely around the campfire." Sargent rescheduled their departure, and Muir and the president spent three splendid days hiking and talking. Afterward Roosevelt supported the recession of the Yosemite Grant and, by proclamation, created five new national parks, twenty-three national monuments and 150 national forests!

Muir knew that his girls were due to reach Crocker's Station about the time he left Yosemite Valley so he sent a letter to them there.

•

Central Hotel
Merced, Cal, May 19th [1903]

My darlings Wanda & Helen,

I hope you had a fine ride into the mountains and that all your trip will be a rich & happy one. Dont try to cross any deep streams.

I had a glorious time with the President. Camped out alone with him 3 nights, in the Sequoia Grove, back of Glacier Point, & at foot of Yosemite near Bridal Veil. Heaven bless you my darlings. Goodbye. Your affectionate father, John Muir

•

On that same day, Wanda wrote home, casually mentioning the epic presidential trip. She must have heard of, but did not mention the annoyance felt by the Yosemite Valley residents and State officials imported for the event. Roosevelt had bypassed the elaborate celebration they had planned in favor of camping out with Muir.

•

Crocker's Station
May 19, 1903

Dear Mama:

We reached here safely last night and will start for Hetch Hetchy day after tomorrow. We had a most delightful trip in with cool weather, fine comfortable stage, good horses and smooth roads. It was snowing a little when we got to Hazel Green, but it didn't seem very cold.[1] The crowd is just fine. Everyone is having a fine time, is jolly and eats and works well. Last night we slept out under a sugar pine and this morning I felt really rested for the first time in over a month. Today we have just loafed and breathed fine air and looked at the pines and the river and been perfectly and absolutely happy . . . no one would ever think that we had been civilized mortals only two days ago . . .

Everything up here is just at its best and there is not so very much snow. The air is fine and I feel as if I could walk fifty or so miles without half trying, but I just lie here and feel happy and have only walked about two or three. The horses come tomorrow. I haven't heard anything from Papa except that the President had struck for the woods and had not been seen by the expectant people in the Valley . . .

We eat as if we hadn't been fed for months and hard tack seems delicious. The cake you sent in was eaten on the stage and seemed vastly better than any cake that had ever been made before. You have made friends for life of all the boys by sending it.

[Wanda]

•

Before he boarded ship in New York, Muir sent a last fatherly note to Wanda and Helen at Crocker's. "How beautiful Hetch Hetchy must be," he commented. "Take no risks of dangerous fords or crumbling cliffs. Heaven bless and keep you, my darlings. When you

1. Hazel Green was a stage stop on the Coulterville Road.

go back to school, don't study too hard.[1] Nothing you can learn there is worth your health . . . Write to me often. Care of Baring Brothers, London, England."

Muir, Sargent and Sargent's son left for England on May 29, 1903. Twelve months later Muir landed alone in San Francisco. During the globe-trotting year, he had seen everything from "endless galleries of paintings . . . Enough for a lifetime . . . " in Paris to "wild gardens" in Russia, to the Himalayas, up the "noble famous old Nile stream . . . " to the "far antipodal Eucalyptus land" of Australia, and "the strange forests, geysers, glaciers, ferny fiords . . . " of New Zealand. After recovering from a devastating bout of ptomaine poisoning in Russia, Muir left the Sargents. From mid-September on, he traveled alone. His powerful friend Harriman smoothed the way, especially aboard his steamship line.

Muir was treated royally, but every letter home—and there were legions of them—confessed homesickness and anxiety for his "Wife & Darlings." Their responses rarely reached him, which increased his concern, particularly for Helen's health. A few times he telegraphed home for reassurance which Louie cabled back. At Christmas, however, when Helen was desperately sick with pneumonia, Muir had no premonition.

Muir's homecoming was triumphant. Wanda and Helen met him at the pier when the ship docked on May 27, 1904. They were amazed to see him sun-tanned and glowing with vitality. After his illness, he had weighed only 100 pounds; now, 148 pounds filled out his frame and clothes. Never before or again was he that heavy. For days his pleased family teased him about his bulk.

During the remainder of 1904, Muir was immersed in answering accumulated correspondence and spearheading the fight to have Yosemite Valley and the Mariposa Grove of Big Trees, a State Grant since 1864, receded to the United States. To win this battle royal, he had to become a lobbyist in Sacramento, and use pressure and friends, particularly Harriman, whose influence and telegrams could alter State votes.

As the work and tension increased, his weight and good humor decreased. When it was time to join the 1904 Sierra Club Outing at Tuolumne Meadows he could not leave, but Wanda and Helen were excited members. Once more, dear Papa advised them to do as he said, not as he had done.

•

1. Both Wanda and Helen attended summer school on the Cal campus at Berkeley, which Wanda found "hard, monotonous work."

Martinez July 14, 1904

Darlings Helen & Wanda.

We were very glad to get your letters assuring us you were well & happy & telling us about your trips to Mono & Mt Dana etc. You should also climb Mt Gibbs if you have time & make notes on the plants, also the big gray broad topped Mammoth Mountain next to Mono Pass on the south. But don't go through the brushy snakey Tuolumne Canon. & don't go up Mt Ritter on account of the miles of ice you would have to travel over.[1] We are all well. Heaven bless you, darlings

John Muir

•

While the year 1905 held one singular triumph for Muir, it was one of tragedy for him and his family. The triumph came on February 25, when a bitterly contested bill, receding the Yosemite Grant to the national government, passed by one vote in the California Senate. Muir reacted with joy and weariness. "And now that the fight is finished and my education as a politician and a lobbyist is finished, I am almost finished myself."

Family life in the "Big House" and college for Wanda, only months short of graduation, were finished also. A doctor advised that Helen must move to a desert area for a year. She had not regained strength after another siege with pneumonia early in the year, and dry air seemed imperative. Wanda was needed, and as always, responded selflessly. She left the university, left her sorority and the attentions of a handsome mining student named Thomas Rea Hanna. Again, her role was that of Big Sister, guardian and companion.

Wanda had met Tom Hanna, scion of prominent families in Gilroy, at the university, which he also attended. At first she was attracted by his good looks and affable, easy-going personality, but it was his respect and solicitude for her that won her heart. It was a heady experience for her to be number one to anyone. Tom shared her affinity for mountains, and had spent several months working as a ranger in Stanislaus National Forest near Yosemite. He was especially interested in mining.

Early in May, Muir, Wanda, Helen, and a nurse left for Arizona. Only Mama, as usual, remained at home, anxiously awaiting letters. Wanda's optimistic one en route must have reassured her.

•

1. Muir never forgot his perilous first ascent of Mount Ritter in 1872.

Somewhere in Nevada
Saturday Morning [May, 1905]

Dear Mama:

We got started safely last night and are having just the very best possible time. The weather is perfect and as there are only two other people in the car besides us four, we have lots of room, and everything just our own way. We have been enjoying the most beautiful views all morning. I hadn't the least idea that we would see so much really truly mountain country. When I woke up this morning we were still in the snow sheds and the car was stuffy and headachy. I couldn't see much, but as soon as I got the window open (much to the porter and conductor's horror), I knew that we were in the mountains for the air had a delicious, snowy snap about it that I have never felt anywhere else. I forgot all about the stuffiness in my head and have been in a constant state of healthy rejoicing ever since even though we are down in the sagebrush country now.

I didn't expect the trip to be so much fun, but its perfectly fine. There was lots of snow around Truckee and that and the sight of the blue mountains gave me a hard attack of mountain craze, just when I thought I was going to be intensely civilized. We opened all the windows and enjoyed ourselves tremendously, but the conductor still thinks we are considerably crazy because we prefer wind off the snow to Pullman car bad air. Maybe we are queer, but we are having a much better time than the lady in the drawing room section who is afraid of drafts, wears diamonds and says in regard to things in general "that it's such a bore, don't you know."

It's time for lunch now so I'll stop and write again tomorrow.

Lovingly,
Wanda

•

Muir had anticipated "a grand healing time" for the "sagebrush orphans" in camps, but because of rainy weather and thanks to a friend's kindness, they stayed instead at a ranch near Wilcox, in southeastern Arizona. Letters from Wanda and Helen elicited a June 15 reply from Louie Muir.

•

Martinez, Calif., June 15, 1905

My darling Wanda,

Your delightful letter just came and though I both laughed and cried over it, there is comfort in it too. I have just found Wilcox on the map and suppose that letters will come from there in about 2 days. O, it seems a long long way, and yet it is always near our own California. Helen's precious letter came day before yesterday and I took it over to Aunt Margaret. She seems pretty well, and said she would try to answer when you wrote . . .

The Will Muirs have the kitchen, dining room, and our old room upstairs![1] To think of it! Ette used the lower east room for her dining room and has a kerosene stove there. No wonder she looked tired after all that moving and shifting about. Uncle David seems pretty well. He gave me some delicious peaches from the tree in the yard.

How I do wish I could send you all the box of glowing red raspberries that Mrs. Boss brought to day. Write if there is anything I can send to you . . .

O my beloved three, if ever loving wishes and earnest prayers can guard and keep you, surely you will have a summer and a winter of good fortune . . .

Keeney seems to be wondering why the place is so silent, though the birds are singing merrily as ever.[2]

The weather is beautiful every morning, but the evenings are almost wintry, with great masses of blue fog rolling over Benicia and Mt. Diablo.

Lum says the Postman is coming so good bye.

Ever lovingly

Mother.

June 21, 1905

My darling Wanda

Two blessed letters yours to day and Helen's yesterday, are here rejoicing us much in the hope that the desert air will be good for you all. The Postman will return soon so I can only write a few lines.

I have readdressed 8 letters for you all to day. I have just found in Helen's desk the paper to Dr. Goddard did you want it sent. I did send the book.

I have been very sick this is the first day I could write since my

1. Will Muir, the only male descendant of the three Muir brothers, was thirty-six when he and his wife moved in with his parents, David and Juliette Muir, in the original Strentzel-Muir home.

2. "Keeney" was one of the successive family dogs named for the original Stickeen.

other letter, but I feel much better and Dr. Rattan says I will be all right soon. It is a great comfort to have Cousin Frances here.

Ah Sam is calling so

Good bye my beloved three,
Mother

•

Three days after Mrs. Muir's letter was mailed, her doctor telegraphed that she was gravely ill. Muir and the girls caught the next train.[1] When they reached home they learned she was suffering from pneumonia, but her basic illness was even more serious. Within days Helen's health worsened, so she had to return to Arizona. A former teacher accompanied her, since, she recorded later, "neither Papa nor Wanda could leave Mama . . . The leave taking from my mother was a terrible thing for both of us. She knew as well as I that we would never see each other again.[2]

Wanda's torment was great also, but, at least, she was home, where she could help and comfort her dying mother. Louie, fifty-eight, lived only until August 6.

An essential part of her husband was buried with her in the Strentzel family graveyard. She had been not only a loving and acutely understanding wife, but a friend, confidante, critic, advisor, and editor as well. As shown in letters, their periodic separations, necessitated by his work and well-being, had strengthened, not weakened, their love and appreciation of each other.

As soon as practical after the funeral, Muir and Wanda rejoined Helen, and moved to Adamana in northeastern Arizona. Muir recorded that the dry desert air was "distinctly, palpably good." He found some solace and interest in the study of the nearby petrified trees. By foot and on horseback, often accompanied by his daughters, he observed several fossil "forests" and added his influence to having them preserved. Ultimately President Roosevelt responded to public advocacy and created the Petrified Forest National Monument.

Nature and Helen's recovery lessened Muir's sorrow. Adamana, a railroad fuel stop, had been founded in 1890. Services were provided so sightseers would have a place to stay while they visited the various forests. Although they had a two-room cabin with a fireplace, built for comfort and privacy, Muir and the girls slept in a tent and had meals at the Stevenson Hotel.

When estate business forced Muir to return to Martinez, he took

1. July 6, 1905, letter from Muir to Theodore P. Lukens.
2. Letter from Helen to Linne Marsh Wolfe, February 1943.

Holt-Atherton Pacific Center for Western Studies

The distinctly "palpably good" desert air of Adamana, Arizona, and the petrified forests nearby healed Helen's lungs and lifted the spirits of all three Muirs. Wanda, John, and Helen on the porch of the hotel where they had meals.

time to study fossils at the university libraries in Berkeley. He reported on his sedentary activities in frequent letters to Helen and Wanda, whose pursuits were far more vigorous. However, Wanda's indoor sport was writing letters not only to "Dear Papa" but also to "Dear Tom," for absence had indeed deepened their love. Muir made allusion to marriage in one of his letters.

•

Martinez, Jan 15, 1906

Darling Girls.

I am wearying for another letter. This is the 3d blank day—no letter, & the 3d day of rain.

I went over to the dismal old home yesterday.[1] Sun had looked after the garret leaks. One tree, a little eucalyptus near the calistema was blown down Saturday night, but Sun cut off the top & set it up again, & also braced up other trees & palms that were badly bent over.

I'm getting dreadfully lonesome & heart-hungry to see you. No matter what friends or husbands you may be blessed with or bothered with you will never have so devoted & devout lover as I am, because I know you best. You are so purely good I should have loved you whether your father or not

O dear, these lonely days!! I must either get into consuming hard work or go up a canon . . .

Heaven guard & bless you forever. So prays

Your loving lonely Dad

May's, Jan. 16, 1906

Darlings.

. . . A heavy S.E. gale is blowing & with slight abatements has been for four days . . . The eucalyptus trees are chanting & clapping their leafy hands gloriously, so are the farmers & merchants & most everybody save a few insane growlers who fear the floods will sweep all the land & life of the State to the sea & are praying deliverance from a wet death. Dont go near that quicksand river! & I do beseech you watch against taking colds & chills every minute. Dry toast your blankets every night & sleep in the cottage whenever

1. Rather than coping alone in his big house, Muir stayed with his niece, May Reid Coleman, and her husband, Arthur, who had a beautiful home north of his own. Coleman was still Muir's business manager.

there is the least hint of any sort of storm. Thus bravely you will fight your way to breezy life giving summer.

I think that the cherry orchard had better be planted to muscat instead of Tokay. I think we can get fine rooted grafted vines from Frank Swett. We have no muscat & too many Tokay are being planted all over the state . . .

I'm keeping the fireside keeping warm & deploring our separation & my mental barrenness, reading & fidgiting but eating & sleeping fairly well & ever turning fondly toward the buttes & coal-bunkers where my heart darlings are so bravely fighting lifes battle . . .

John Muir

Feb. 28th, '06

Dear Papa:

Your letter and the deeds came this morning.

You speak of almond blossoms and spring weather. I had forgotten that this was the time for them, but it made me awfully homesick to think of them. Here we are having another sandstorm. Such a bad one that it is hard even to see the coal bunkers. However Helen seems to feel pretty well, so I guess we can stand it. But I think it would make even a saint cross. I have a toothache besides so I'm not very amiable.

Everything else is about as usual.

When are you coming back? Soon, I hope. It's too bad that you can't get the inheritance tax settled this time, but I suppose there is no hurry about it.

The freight bill for the Goldberg box has come and we will give the box itself a cordial welcome.[1]

Lovingly,
Wanda.

1. Muir sent the girls box after box from Goldberg Bowen's in San Francisco, containing "canned meats and sardines . . . olives . . . crackers . . . cookies . . . orange marmalade (from Dundee, Scotland) and dried fruits . . . nuts and candy. Sometimes a box of oranges or apples or fresh pineapples and fresh coconuts . . ." [Helen Muir to Linnie Marsh Wolfe, Feb., 1943.]

•

In April Wanda and her father traded places, and she returned joyfully to Martinez to see Tom Hanna, make wedding plans, and have dental work done. As had Muir, she stayed with the Colemans and, from there, witnessed and described the earthshaking event of April 18, 1906.

•

May's April 18, 1906

Dear Papa:

At five o'clock this morning the worst earthquake ever known here struck Alhambra Valley and left the houses in it a wreck. Every one of our five chimneys (our own at the big house) are down, the roof is torn up, all the mantels except the parlour one, are entirely smashed and a great deal of the plastering is down. Nothing else is much hurt. Your books and papers are alright and so are our pictures. But I never saw such a smash in my life. The whole house has to be rebuilt.[1] What shall I do? Hadn't I better get back to Arizona as soon as possible and let you come up and see what has to be done?

May's new house has all the plastering off downstairs and both chimneys are down and one side of the porch.

Aunt Margaret's house is moved eight inches off the foundation and the chimney is down, but there is not much damage inside and she is alright but I don't know where she will go while it is being fixed for they can't have a fire in there now.

The only house in the valley that is not hurt is the adobe.[2] Didn't hurt it at all except a little plaster in front. Most all of Martinez is in ruins. There are rumors of awful things in San Francisco, but as all the telegraph wires are down and there are no trains running I don't know how true they are.

I don't know when this letter will go, but I'll write it so you will know as soon as possible that we are all well and so you can come up

1. Damage was not as extensive as Wanda feared. Only the chimneys in the Muir home required rebuilding, and two rooms needed replastering.

2. This fine-looking, two-story home was built by Don Ygnacio Martinez in 1849. Dr. Strentzel bought it in 1874 and built his home on a hill to the east of the adobe. Now it is part of the John Muir National Historic Site, and is open to the public. During the early years of their marriage, Wanda and Tom Hanna lived in the old adobe.

if you think it best. I wish you could come while I'm here if it is possible for you to leave Helen long enough. Unless you tell me something to the contrary I will start back to Adamana as soon as my teeth will let me, probably a week from today. I've been going to the dentist for the last three weeks and am not through yet, though I hope I will be soon.

Tell Helen that her guitar and the rest of her belongings are safe and unhurt.

I'll write again when I find out how things really are and when I get calmed down a little.[1]

Lovingly, Wanda

•

Soon after the earthquake, Muir returned to survey the damage, and do further research on what he called "enchanted carboniferous forests" in the paleontology archives at the University of California. Even though her wedding date was set for June, ever-faithful Wanda went back to Adamana to be Helen's companion.

•

Adamana, Arizona, June 6, 1906

Dear Papa:

Your last Sunday's letter reached us this morning. I'm afraid you are working entirely too hard in that stuffy old library. It's awful to let yourself get still thinner just before coming down here where you can't get the right sort of things to eat. Even Sig isn't worth getting sick for.

It has been cold and dusty and now it is very hot and dusty here, but Helen and I are both feeling fine, but are badly burned and freckled.

There have been only a few people here lately, but day before yesterday I took three people out to the third forest. Had a fine trip and the team came in as gaily as they started.[2]

Did you answer the Santa Fe people's questions about the Blue Forest? Mr. Stevenson has had several letters from them about the

1. Instead of calming down, Wanda took the first train to Berkeley and "was among the first to volunteer at the evacuation hospital . . . Despite lack of training, on the sixth day she was in charge of the hospital as head nurse." ["Wanda Muir Hanna," mss. by Greta Variel]

2. Both Wanda and Helen loved to drive tourists in a stage to the Petrified Forests.

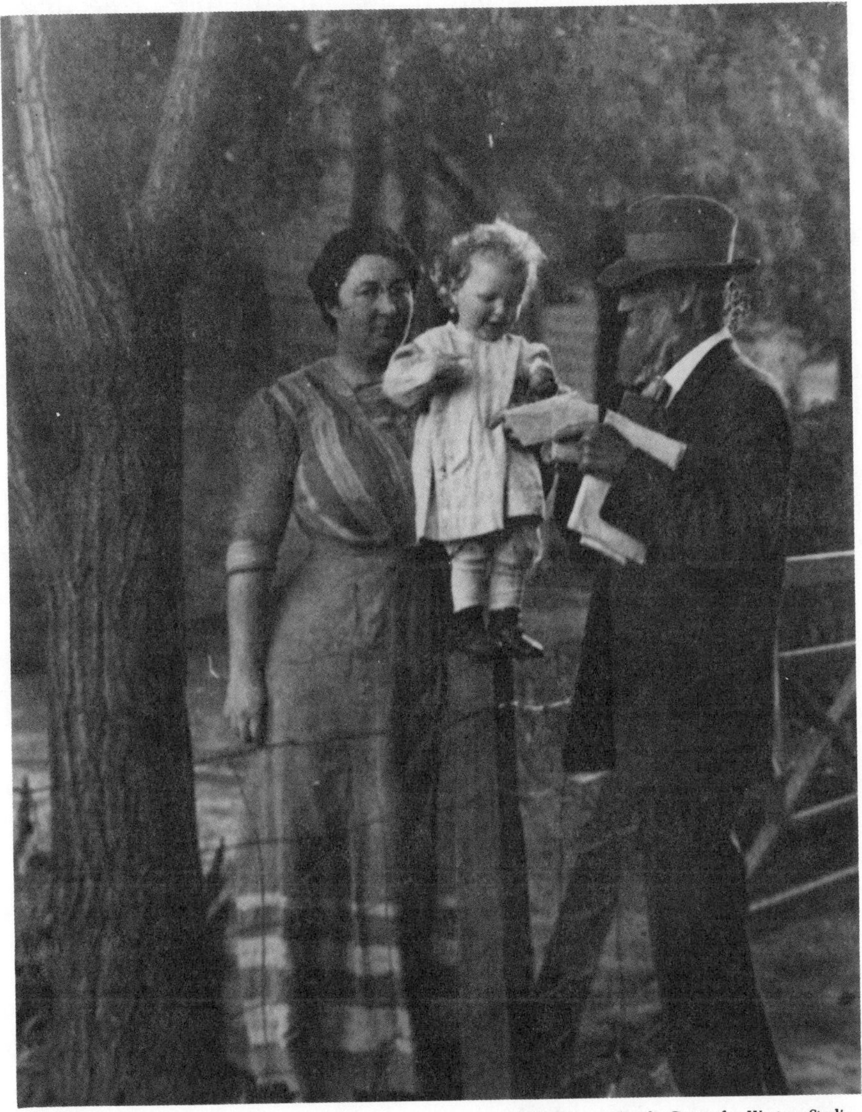

Holt-Atherton Pacific Center for Western Studies

Richard Rea Hanna was the third of Muir's nine grandsons, five by Wanda, and four by Helen.

Bad Lands.[1] So I think they must be going to advertise all the Adamana attractions.

Mr. Fiske sent you some most beautiful views of Yosemite.[2] They are very large mounted photographs that would be fine framed.

I am glad to hear that you have collected some money and that May's house is again in order.

I don't think you need to worry about Tom not taking charge of the ranch, for he intends to and I think by next January you will see us in the adobe.[3] I'll try to help Helen all I can with her housekeeping. She is very anxious to have the big house fixed up and insists that by having the sweeping and hardest work done, she can take care of it alright, and I think she can.[4] If she can't I'll do it for her, either in the big house or somewhere else.

I think I will have to start back on the tenth but Dora is going to sleep out in the cottage so Helen won't be so entirely alone and as she is feeling so well I don't think there would be the least use in your coming down for such a short time.

If the train is on time I will see you on the eleventh at 4:30

•

Because the "big house" was still disrupted by earthquake damage, Wanda and Tom were married at the Coleman's home on June 20. Only a few family members and intimate friends attended. John Muir gave the bride away, in more ways than one. No longer could he count on her as a constant support.

Although many more letters were exchanged between the two before his death on December 24, 1914, it seems fitting to conclude this volume with Wanda's first as a married woman.

•

1. There are six separate forests in the present, enlarged national park. Helen Muir said that her father named one the Blue Forest because the wood was blue. The Santa Fe Railroad publicity department wanted information to use in promotional material about the forests which are part of Arizona's Painted Desert. So-called arid "badlands" were caused by erosion.

2. Photographer George Fiske, an old friend of Muir's, had a studio and home in Yosemite Valley.

3. The Hannas lived in the adobe until their family, ultimately six children, crowded it. After Muir's death, they moved into the original Strentzel home where Wanda had spent her first eight years. Tom Hanna worked for his father-in-law.

4. Louie Muir had willed the "big house," left to her by her parents, to Helen.

Crocker's Station
Sequoia, Cal. July 9, 1906

Dear Papa:

From Tuolumne where I wrote to Helen from last, we went to Headquarters Camp on Cherry River and from there to Lake Eleanor[1] and now we are at Crockers on our way to Yosemite.

We are having a glorious trip, just going where we want to, when we want to, without any definite plans, and camping wherever we happen to be. I had the best time of all at Lake Eleanor. I'll be so glad when you and Helen can get up here in the pines again. It doesn't seem possible that your desert air is better for anyone than this fine fragrant air. I wish you could come up here this fall or to the Lake. There is a nice clean cottage that Helen could stay in if it rained, and as many trout as anyone can eat, and fine piney air, and the beautiful clear lake with the snow capped mountains beyond.

From Yosemite [Valley] we will probably go up to Tuolumne Meadows for a few days, then back to the Lake and then down to the lowlands for the building of chimneys.

When do you intend to come back to the [Alhambra] Valley? I suppose I'll know when I get to Yosemite and read the letters from you that I hope are waiting for me there. I haven't heard anything from you since I was married. It still seems a little queer to be spoken of as Mrs. Hanna, especially when I am told, as I was once, that "Miss Muir was to be married" and am asked if I ever met Miss Muir.

We have two fine horses to ride and a dandy little black mule to pack, but we have also done a good deal of walking besides. The flowers everywhere are in full bloom, and it's good to see them again, but the sugar pines are the best of all! . . .

I'm so anxious to hear how things are going in Adamana and especially how you and Helen are standing the hotness there. How's the grub? Wish I could send you some trout.

Our next address will be Tuolumne. You better put "hold till called for" on the envelope and write often.

Did you see the article in the National Magazine about the Petri-

---

1. Within a couple of years, Cherry River and Lake Eleanor, named for Josiah D. Whitney's daughter, became integral parts of the water development surrounding the damming of Hetch Hetchy Valley. Muir fought that desecration vehemently but unsuccessfully, and the defeat saddened his last year.

fied Forest, the Bad Lands (which the man hadn't seen) and the Muir family? I found the magazine in the Lake Eleanor blacksmith shop and read about driving out to the forest. There is a picture of me with Helen's name under it.

Please remember me to all my Adamana friends.

Lovingly, your very happy daughter,

Wanda Muir Hanna

Afterword

It was Jean Hanna Clark's wish that the letters between her mother and grandfather be followed by an epilogue so readers would know of Wanda Muir Hanna's contributions in maturity as an exceptional individual—a mother, businesswoman, and civic leader. Jean had made episodic notes for such an account, many of which are included in the subsequent text.

Muir, who had only two daughters, must have been astonished and pleased at the number of sons—nine—they produced. Helen, who lived and thrived in desert areas most of her life, married a man named Buel Funk and they had four boys: Muir, Stanley, Walter and John. After Funk's death, the family name was changed legally to Muir except for the first-born, who didn't want the duplication. Only Walter Muir had a child, and that a girl, so the Muir name is in danger of dying out, but not the progeny. The descendants of Wanda Muir and Tom Hanna include 17 great-grandchildren and 23 great-great-grandchildren.

Wanda and Tom loved children and had six, five sons and a daughter: Strentzel, John, Richard, Robert, Jean Louise, and Ross. The brood crowded first the adobe and then the original Strentzel home in Alhambra Valley. Nevertheless, Jean said, her parents found room in their hearts and home to include several other young men. They shared when things were plentiful, and stretched the soup and beans (and oatmeal, which was *always* plentiful) when times were hard. They weathered crises, tragedies, and the great depression. In fact, "there has never been an accurate account of the boys . . . who shared the hospitality of the Hanna home." Wanda and Tom became legal guardians of Leonard, Jose, and George; others like Toji, Ben, and Dave stayed for months or years.

In addition, the Hannas befriended troubled teenagers, and encouraged and tutored foreigners intent on becoming American citizens. Needy families were remembered at the holiday season even, Jean recalled, "when the fare was rather skimpy at home."

Besides managing and working the extensive orchards in Alhambra Valley, the Hannas grazed cattle and horses on the adjacent hills and in the Crockett area. Both were active in the real estate business, especially in subdividing and building on the Strentzel-Muir property near the town of Crockett, several miles from Martinez. Coincident with that development, following World War I, Wanda and Tom owned and operated a lumber yard in Berkeley. "They were full partners in all endeavors, both business and domestic," recalls their son, Richard Rea Hanna.

From 1920 until 1937, Tom spent a great deal of time working on the May Lundy mine in Lundy Canyon on the east side of the Sierra. A rough winter, an avalanche, and inadequate financing caused its closure in 1937. The whole family mourned, but retained several lots and continued, as several still do, to spend vacations in the canyon they know and love.

The Hannas' hard work and ambitions were devastated by the 1929 stock market crash, the resultant Great Depression, rising land taxes, and legal suits which followed the condemnation of their property abutting the Carquinez Bridge. Despite the reversals, Tom and Wanda provided food and housing to their own and foster children, and financed college educations for their five boys. Jean, however, had to work her way through business school and became a top-notch secretary. At the time of her death in 1976, she was confidential secretary to the governor of Nevada.

"In the strict interpretation of the word," Jean wrote, "my mother and dad were 'permissive parents.' They seldom told us 'no' unless there was a good explanation, and they had such confidence in us, we were allowed to do almost anything we wanted badly enough. For instance, beginning in their pre-teens, the boys went on pack trips in the Sierra, unchaperoned except for their animals. They traveled to Yosemite, Mount Lassen, Mount Rainier, and other places, stopping at farmhouses and sleeping in barns or camping along the way.

"Of course, the Hannas were greatly criticized by their neighbors just as my grandfather Muir had been," Jean continued, "but those were wonderful, carefree, happy, uninhibited days and they were hardy, capable boys." At the same time they indulged in such independence, the brothers developed even more self-reliance and responsibility. And, of course, they were following in their grandfather's footsteps. In addition to such autonomous ventures, the family as a whole enjoyed numerous camping trips, particularly those to Lundy Canyon where the boys helped their father in the mine.

Wanda was always involved in Martinez affairs, often in important though volunteer positions. She was a trustee of the Alhambra Union High School, a director of the Contra Costa Public Health Association, a secretary of the Alhambra Valley Farm Center, a member of the California Federation of Women's Clubs, and naturally the Sierra Club, plus the local real estate board and the women's club. During P.T.A. meetings, she participated, but kept her hands busy mending socks. Feeding her family, housekeeping, and selling real estate filled her days, but, sometimes, she took time out to play her violin. No longer did she have to play in a secluded, sound-proof room, but anywhere she pleased.

She was a good violinist, Jean thought. "Not outstanding, but she enjoyed her instrument, and rainy, or dismal, foggy days became special when she played some of her old, favorite classics. She exposed all of us to music, but, unfortunately, only Ross displayed any talent. One of the thrills of Mother's life was the day he played a trumpet solo, 'Carnival of Venice,' in a high school music contest. The audience gave him a standing ovation, and tears welled in Mother's eyes, then and whenever she spoke of it."

Going to a circus was another passion of Wanda's. She had not seen one until after she left home at nineteen, but from then on, Jean recorded, "Mother never missed a chance to load up the old Hupmobile with youngsters, tour through the back roads of Contra Costa County to west Oakland where the huge circus tent was. We climbed up the rickety bleachers, and watched every move of the tight rope walkers and the acrobats, the animals and the clowns. Mother was known to cancel some very important appointments in favor of the sawdust treat."

Wanda and Tom's love for each other never faltered, and they cherished their children, blood and foster, who matured into upstanding adults. "School problems, world affairs, politics were all discussed openly," was Jean's comment, "especially around the huge dining room table. Startling topics were occasionally mentioned, but everyone had a chance to express himself, and all questions, no matter how sensitive, were answered freely and openly."

Wanda, Muir's "bloom baby," and the girl he said was "unstoppable as an avalanche" continued to achieve and contribute but only until she was 61. On July 29, 1942, she died after an emergency appendectomy, and her body was interred in the family graveyard with "Dear Papa and Dear Mama." Sister Helen, whose youthful health had been so perilous, outlived her by 22 years.

Tom Hanna was desolated by Wanda's death, and, although he worked as an engineer on pipelines in Canada and Alaska during World War II, and traveled widely, he was always lonely. He survived her by just five years.

After Wanda's death, Greta Variel, her sorority sister, wrote a moving memorial. In it, she noted that tenderness and strength were wedded in Wanda, that she could be both dynamic and a haven of peace, "a fountain of wisdom and good sense." Nearly half a century later, Wanda's spirit and many of her fine characteristics live on in the Muir-Hanna families.

Index

Since Wanda, Helen, Louie and John Muir appear on virtually every page of this book, they are not included in the index.